# TERRORISM WITH CHEMICAL

# AND BIOLOGICAL WEAPONS

## CALIBRATING RISKS

## AND RESPONSES

# TERRORISM WITH CHEMICAL

# AND BIOLOGICAL WEAPONS

## CALIBRATING RISKS

## AND RESPONSES

### EDITED BY BRAD ROBERTS

THE CHEMICAL AND BIOLOGICAL ARMS CONTROL INSTITUTE
ALEXANDRIA, VA

Terrorism with Chemical and Biological Weapons:
Calibrating Risks and Responses
© 1997 by the Chemical and Biological Arms Control Institute
Alexandria, VA 22314
Printed in the United States of America

Cover design by Sarah Carter
Typesetting by Free Hand Press, Inc.

ISBN 0-9656168-0-0

Chemical and Biological Arms Control Institute
2111 Eisenhower Avenue, Suite 302
Alexandria, VA 22314
Tel: 703-739-1538
Fax: 703-739-1525

# Contents

# About the Authors

**James Adams** is Washington bureau chief of the London *Sunday Times*. He reports on U.S. politics, international relations, terrorism, and intelligence matters. He is the author of twelve books, including *The Financing of Terror*.

**Anthony Fainberg** is a consultant and national security analyst. From 1985 to 1995 he served as senior associate at the Congressional Office of Technology Assessment, where he specialized on terrorism, proliferation, and technology.

**Brian M. Jenkins** is deputy chairman of Kroll Associates, an international investigative and consulting firm. He served previously as chairman of RAND's political science department and director of its research on political violence. He is the author of *International Terrorism: A New Mode of Conflict* and editor-in-chief of *TVI Report*, a quarterly journal dealing with terrorism, violence, and insurgency.

**Karl Lowe** is an analyst at the Institute for Defense Analyses in Alexandria, Virginia. A retired Army colonel since 1993, he has authored a series of studies for the Office of the Secretary of Defense and Defense Intelligence Agency on biological warfare concerns. He previously served as chief of the Joint Staff's Strategy Division, chief of the Army Staff's Conventional Arms Control Division, and advisor on national security strategy to the Under Secretary of Defense for Policy during the Bush Administration.

**JOSEPH F. PILAT** is a policy analyst with the Los Alamos National Laboratory, where he works in the Nonproliferation and International Security Division, with expertise on nuclear proliferation, arms control, and terrorism. He is the author or editor of numerous books, including *1995: A New Beginning for the NPT*.

**RON PURVER** is a strategic analyst specializing in proliferation with the Canadian Security Intelligence Service. He has also served as research director of the Canadian Centre for Arms Control and Disarmament in Ottawa. In 1995, he authored a study entitled *Chemical and Biological Terrorism: The Threat According to the Open Literature*.

**BRAD ROBERTS** is a member of the research staff of the Institute for Defense Analyses, where he specializes on issues of proliferation, nonproliferation, and counterproliferation. He is also chairman of the CBACI Research Advisory Council and an adjunct professor at George Washington University. He is the author or editor of many publications, including *Biological Weapons: Weapons of the Future?*

**JONATHAN B. TUCKER** is director for chemical and biological weapons proliferation issues at the Center for Nonproliferation Studies of the Monterey Institute of International Studies. He served previously with the Arms Control and Disarmament Agency and the Congressional Office of Technology Assessment.

**FRANK YOUNG** retired in May 1996 as director of the Office of Emergency Preparedness in the Public Health Service of the Department of Health and Human Services. He served previously as a member of the World Health Organization's Commission on Health and the Environment and as dean of the School of Medicine and Dentistry at the University of Rochester.

# PREFACE

On March 20, 1995, a Japanese religious cult attacked the Tokyo subway system using the nerve gas sarin. The international community's immediate response to the attack was a global search for answers to questions unfamiliar to most people: What is sarin? How easy or hard is it to make? How does it compare with other poison gases that have been used as weapons? Why have such weapons not been used by terrorists before? How do we protect ourselves against them? Is the United States prepared for such an attack in this country?

In the surge of media commentary on the Tokyo attack, exaggeration was far too common; in-depth understanding far too rare. An effective response to the challenge of terrorists' use of chemical and biological weapons begins with a better understanding of the issues involved. To that end, the Chemical and Biological Arms Control Institute (CBACI) produced this monograph through a generous grant from the Sarah Scaife Foundation and under the leadership of Brad Roberts, chairman of the institute's Research Advisory Council and a member of the Board of Trustees. *Terrorism with Chemical and Biological Weapons: Calibrating Risks and Responses* is a sophisticated, nuanced, and balanced assessment of the threat of chemical and biological terrorism. Its conclusion should be cause for neither complacency nor despair: the threat is real, but the international community has the ability—if it has the will—to combat it effectively.

This monograph is the first such study of this length that CBACI has had the privilege to publish. On behalf of CBACI, I extend my thanks to those who helped us achieve this milestone: the Sarah Scaife Foundation for its support of the project; staff member Leslie Rodrigues for her work in organizing the conference at which some of these materials were presented and in pulling together the draft;

Martha Membrino for her editing and production coordination; and Brad Roberts, not only for his leadership on the project and as editor of this volume, but for his strong support of the institute from the day it opened its doors.

Michael Moodie
President

# Introduction

## Brad Roberts

This monograph has its genesis in the events surrounding the nefarious chemical attack on the Tokyo subway system by the Aum Shinrikyo sect. In the way of Washington, the events created great media interest, which precipitated telephone calls to local experts by journalists, which forced those of us affiliated with the Chemical and Biological Arms Control Institute to come to grips with what we thought we knew about the terrorism subject and its chemical and biological dimensions. The subsequent bombing in Oklahoma City reinforced the urgency of the task.

In the ensuing weeks and months, we turned to the literature on terrorism and to the work of colleagues in the academic world. Our discoveries were enlightening if disappointing. That literature devotes little attention to the potential use by terrorists of weapons of mass destruction. In one sense, the relative scarcity of material is understandable—analysts have been reluctant to publish descriptions of societal vulnerabilities to and the technical attributes of possible new instruments of terrorist violence, for fear of planting those ideas in the minds of evildoers. In another sense, however, the scarcity has reflected disinterest—analysts have tended to focus on what terrorists have done instead of what they might have done or might do in the future.

What limited attention has been given to terrorism with weapons of mass destruction has focused almost exclusively on the use of nuclear and radiological devices, with matters chemical and biological typically treated as a lesser-included category. To the extent there has been any thinking about the chemical and biological aspect, it has tended to emphasize the impact of technology diffusion on the prospects for terrorism. The fact that ever more individuals, groups, and states have access to the materials and technology of chemical and biological weapons has led to dire predictions about the imminence of massively destructive terrorist attacks. But these predictions are at stunning odds with the historical record: of all of the terrorist actions of recent years and decades, only the Aum subway attack has actually employed such weapons. How are we to understand this disparity between prediction and experience? Is it merely an historical coincidence and, if so, should we anticipate a wave of terrorist attacks employing chemical or biological agents? Or are there explanations that lead to a less apocalyptic view of the future?

In a search for answers to these questions, we decided that it was necessary to probe beyond conventional wisdoms and to lead a process of inquiry and debate among interested scholars and policymakers. This became a research project under CBACI auspices, under my direction in my capacity as chairman of the institute's Research Advisory Council. We set out to answer four basic questions.

First, was 1995 a watershed year? Many pundits have argued that the attacks in Tokyo and Oklahoma City signal a new era in terrorism, one marked by more massively destructive and indiscriminate attacks with heretofore taboo weaponry. The bombing of the World Trade Center in New York a couple of years earlier was frequently cited as confirming this interpretation of events. Our goal was to evaluate these propositions. Are they valid? If so, why? If not, why not?

Second, how important are loosening constraints on the terrorist use of chemical and biological weapons? There are two types of constraints: technical and political. We set out to gain a better understanding of those constraints, of the ways in which they are changing, and of the implications of those changes.

Third, is the taboo really broken? What was or is the taboo vis-à-vis chemical and biological weapons? On whom is that taboo operative? In what ways might it not have broken?

Fourth, what are the appropriate tasks of policy in the light of new circumstances? Here, we set out to bring the big picture into focus for those not already immersed in the process. Where do our priorities lie? How much emphasis do they deserve? What can policy reasonably be expected to contribute to amelioration of this problem, and what can it not be expected to contribute? And what are the future risks of failing now to implement an appropriate agenda?

This volume is the result of this process of inquiry and debate. Our purpose is to disaggregate the topic, examine these specific aspects, frame some arguments, and test some propositions. The materials included here were presented in preliminary form for critical review to a conference on April 29, 1996. We expected a turnout of 50 participants but had nearly 200—surely a sign of the heightened salience of the topic after the events of 1995. The chapters included here by James Adams, Anthony Fainberg, and Joseph Pilat are overview pieces, intended to capture the main themes of discussion of specific questions. The other chapters reflect pieces of work that we particularly wanted to capture for the record. The style and content of the chapters differ markedly, and no effort has been made to wring out the differences for the sake of consistency—the similarities and differences in perspective, interpretation, and recommendation are themselves interesting and valuable. In addition to these written contributions, we benefited from excellent oral presentations by Kathleen Bailey, Steve Emerson, Brendon Hammer, Michael Jakub, Harvey McGeorge, and John Sopko. In my concluding chapter I have set out to distill the key ideas and insights yielded by the process to produce a summary of what was learned.

This volume is being published after our own internal debate about the wisdom of disseminating the discussions of vulnerabilities and technologies included here. Past practice by the terrorism studies community, after all, has limited such dissemination for the reasons cited above. But having witnessed the ebb and flow of hysteria in response to recent terrorist events, the urgency among policymakers to set some proper plans in motion, and steadily growing public interest in the issues, we have opted for publication. The Aum Shinrikyo attack has already underscored the societal vulnerabilities and technical possibilities associated with chemical and biological terrorism. We hope that we can be helpful in putting those into perspective and identifying the necessary actions of governments.

As project director, I owe a debt of gratitude to Michael Moodie for the opportunity to lead this inquiry and to the staff of CBACI for their support of the effort. Special thanks are due to Leslie Rodrigues for excellent administrative and research support. I wish also to express my thanks to the authors for their hard labor and responsiveness to the reactions of others. We hope that our contribution to understanding the chemical and biological terrorism problem will merit the investment of time and effort to review these materials.

# Prospects for NBC Terrorism after Tokyo

## Joseph F. Pilat

T he threat of terrorism involving nuclear, biological, and chemical (NBC) weapons generally has been regarded as low. Recent developments, from reports of nuclear smuggling out of the former Soviet Union, to the terrorist use of nerve gas in a crowded Tokyo subway, to the rapid diffusion of technologies applicable to the manufacture of biological weapons, have heightened fear of the NBC terrorist threat to national and international security. The bombings at the World Trade Center in New York and at the Federal Office Building in Oklahoma City, coupled with Director of Central Intelligence (DCI) John Deutch's assessment of growth in international terrorism, have raised the issue of domestic vulnerability to NBC terrorism in congressional and other circles.[1]

A national reexamination of the issue of NBC terrorism will be undertaken and, in some respects, has already begun with recent Senate hearings.[2] NBC terrorist threat assessments are essential, if politically charged. Responding to NBC terrorism, and the preparations it requires, will not be sustainable over time unless the activities undertaken address realistic threats and can truly prevent, neutralize, or mitigate those threats. Given this perspective, to ensure that the current reexamination of NBC terrorism issues leads to effective measures to deal with the problems at hand, it will be essential to better understand and characterize the threat; to analyze the military and especially the civilian vulnerabilities of the United States, its friends, and its allies; and to assess political, technical, organizational, and operational responses to the threat.

## NBC TERRORISM AFTER TOKYO

There have been periods over the last two decades when, in the view of both academic and policy circles, NBC terrorism was expected to pose a clear and present threat. The focus of these fears was nuclear terrorism, and was primarily driven by growing availability in civilian fuel cycles around the world of materials useful for making weapons. These fears were never realized, and until the Aum Shinrikyo's attack on the Tokyo subway system, no significant acts of NBC terrorism had occurred. Nonetheless, many believed that NBC terrorism was inevitable and that it was only a question of time before a major incident occurred. From this perspective, the Tokyo attack was a confirmation of their sobering prediction. And the use of nerve gas by a group that was also investigating biological and nuclear options has reinforced for many the inevitability of NBC terrorism. It is argued that the use of a chemical agent will inevitably lead to biological and nuclear terrorism because, in part, terrorist organizations will seek a full complement of NBC capabilities. The unprecedented use of such weapons by a person or organization, it is argued, removes the threat of NBC terrorism from the realm of theory to that of practice and effectively ends the taboo on this particularly destructive form of terrorism.

This perspective, which is probably the predominant view of the meaning of the Tokyo attack, should not be dismissed out of hand. Nonetheless, it is probably overblown, and certainly premature. It ignores or under emphasizes key aspects of the attack.

The Tokyo subway attack did not involve mass destruction. It claimed 12 lives; however tragic, this attack was not as deadly as many conventional terrorist attacks, and therefore it raises questions about what threshold was actually crossed by the action. That the terrorists apparently intended to kill more people should not be forgotten or underplayed. However, the fact that their intentions were not realized means that we have not yet experienced terrorism that has brought about mass destruction and that projections about the impact of such terrorism remain speculative.

The attack may have been seen primarily in terms of old patterns of terrorism, as is perhaps suggested by the limited public reaction beyond Japan. Although there were widespread reactions of horror and revulsion to the attack, they were not on the scale that had been predicted for such an event. The Tokyo attack did not really lead to fundamental changes in the way the world is dealing with the threat, although the attack has sensitized publics and governments to the potential dangers of NBC terrorism and has spurred efforts in Japan and the United States, at least, to combat this threat. In Japan, for example, additional video surveillance in subway stations and upgraded fire department capabilities to analyze gases have been put into place, and large-scale gas escape drills have been conducted since the attack. There are reportedly lingering feelings of fear and uncertainty, and some criticism of the government's response to the attack one year later.

The issue of the response and its impact on future actions is critical. The police response in rounding up the organizers of the incident was apparently efficient. Although several suspects remain at large, there does not appear to be a continuing threat from the group. While the effectiveness of the Japanese response can only be judged after the trials of Aum's leader and other activists are completed, the lesson to would-be perpetrators may be that NBC terrorism can lead to the destruction of the organization that perpetrates it. There has not been a spate of copycat attacks in the year since the Tokyo incident, but there may be groups planning such actions.

The long-term impact of the Tokyo incident may be limited by the fact that the agent used by Aum in its attack was chemical rather than biological or nuclear. The use of chemicals does not necessarily mean that other weapons of mass destruction are more likely to be used by terrorists; in fact, it is increasingly recognized that chemical weapons are very different from nuclear and biological weapons in terms of their capabilities. The broader socio-political impact of chemical weapons—their effects on politics in the United States and around the world—may differ as well for a world that has witnessed chemical attacks and threats in the two Gulf Wars and the Bhopal chemical accident in India.

Finally, the terrorist attack was undertaken by a new type of terrorist; the group responsible may have been unique in combining scientific expertise, political-military connections, and wealth with an apocalyptic philosophy. Would all of these characteristics be necessary for an organization to undertake NBC terrorism effectively? Certainly they are important, yet how many other organizations have similar capabilities? To what extent does it matter for the future of NBC terrorism?

Although none of these considerations is, in itself, decisive, they raise questions that are currently unanswerable and they all weigh against early conclusions that the Tokyo attack augurs the shape of things to come. All of these considerations suggest reasons to believe that the implications of the Tokyo attack for future NBC terrorism remain unclear, but that the attack was probably not the watershed that many assume. Nonetheless, the attack should be taken seriously, and there are certain developments that suggest such attacks could occur again in the future.

# CHANGING PATTERNS OF INTERNATIONAL TERRORISM

Since 1968, patterns of international terrorism suggest that terrorists have most often preferred simple acts that either have not produced casualties or have produced only small numbers of casualties. They have rarely attacked defended facilities or sites. This pattern, to the extent it continues, would be inconsistent with most of the actions encompassed by NBC terrorism. However, as will be shown, some patterns are changing.

The shift in terrorism over the last decade or so, and especially since the end of the Cold War, from actions by ideological left-wing terrorists and national separatists to actions by the ideological right, ethnic and religious fundamentalists, and single-issue terrorists has not yet resulted in fundamental changes in terrorist behavior that would inevitably increase the threat of NBC terrorism. But, to the extent that these groups are removed from the promotion of political causes and are pursuing such vague ends as revenge or apocalyptic visions, the prospects of their turning to NBC terrorism increase, but by no means inevitably. From this perspective, let us consider some key changes in terrorist behavior. Notwithstanding the media attention given to and the political impact of more sophisticated and spectacular terrorist operations, most terrorist incidents have been simple in conception and operation. Yet terrorists have become more sophisticated over time, and they can be expected to become more sophisticated in the future with respect to the weapons they employ, the operations they undertake, and the targets they choose.[3] Whether the increasing appeal of such high technology terrorism translates into a greater likelihood of NBC terrorism is a matter of speculation. NBC terrorism, with the prospects of unprecedented deaths, could create mass panic on a scale hitherto unimagined. But terrorists have not yet brought about this level of destruction by their actions. And in the future they may not wish to kill large numbers of people indiscriminately.

To date, as indicated, the great majority of terrorist incidents have either caused no casualties or only limited casualties. Nevertheless, it should be noted that the number of incidents apparently aimed at causing casualties, including assassinations and bombings, has increased since 1975, with a dramatic rise in the 1980s. This increase in casualties and casualty-producing incidents is especially significant. Although terrorist operations producing mass casualties have been extremely rare, and the largest number of deaths produced by these incidents has been on the order of a few hundreds rather than a thousand, ten thousand, or a hundred thousand, there is evidence suggesting that terrorists may now believe that casualties are necessary to generate the amount of publicity formerly evoked by less violent operations. In this vein, although terrorists have only rarely indiscriminately threatened and killed large numbers of people, they may feel pressure to change. We have already seen some evidence to suggest this is occurring. Terrorists could be altering their tactics or their targets and moving toward a higher order of violence than they have been willing to undertake in the past.[4]

Reflecting these new patterns, DCI Deutch sees the terrorist threat as increasing in the post-Cold War era and argues that "terrorists have become increasingly capable, lethal, and wide ranging. Their operating methods and technological expertise—in bomb-making and other skills—are more sophisticated. Terrorist attacks today are more deadly than in the past."[5] One key difference, according to Deutch, is that "Where once terrorists undertook relatively small operations aimed at attaining specific political objectives, today they are more likely to inflict mass casualties as a form of punishment or revenge."[6] The appeal of NBC terrorism could increase as the terrorists' need for publicity increases, as their present tactics become less effective, or as they become desperate. Indeed, Deutch directly expressed this concern:

> We are concerned that terrorists will push this trend to its most awful extreme by employing weapons of mass destruction. Indeed, the prospects for chemical and biological terrorism will increase with the spread of dual-use technologies and expertise. Many of the technologies and materials associated with these programs have legitimate civilian or military applications. Trade in such materials cannot be banned. For example, chemicals used to make nerve agents are also used to make plastics and process foodstuffs. And any modern pharmaceutical facility can produce biological warfare agents as easily as vaccines or antibiotics. The Japanese cult Aum Shinrikyo was able to legally obtain all components needed to build the massive chemical infrastructure that produced the poison gas released in the Tokyo subway. The use of nuclear materials is less likely, but in December we saw terrorists employ radioactive material for the first time, when Chechen rebels planted radioactive material in a public park in Moscow.[7]

Deutch's analysis of the shifts in terrorism is largely correct, but it should be noted that we have been observing this shift for more than a decade. It has not yet resulted in a wave of NBC terrorism, and there is little reason to believe it will do so in the future. Most terrorists whose behavior is driven by such motives as punishment and revenge have not shown an interest in weapons of mass destruction. To date, an apocalyptic group has been the only one that has undertaken a significant act of NBC terrorism, and such groups are the most likely candidates to use such means in the future. Indeed, NBC terrorism does constitute "the most awful extreme" of the patterns Deutch outlined. They suggest that NBC terrorism may be more likely than in the past, but is by no means inevitable or likely to become prevalent. The two concrete actions he refers to did not involve mass destruction; indeed, the Chechen "action" was not carried out and its effects would have been largely insignificant had it been implemented.

## Why NBC Terrorism Is Not Widespread

Despite recent events and these changing terrorist patterns, NBC terrorism is not widespread, and it may never be as common as conventional terrorist actions. The prospects for widespread NBC terrorism are unclear, in large part because there remain technical and political obstacles to NBC terrorism. Although the chemical and biological activities of Aum highlight the declining technological barriers to NBC terrorism, which is also demonstrated in the nuclear sphere by reports of nuclear smuggling from the former Soviet Union, the fate of Aum may actually reinforce a key political barrier to NBC terrorism. This analysis focuses on two sets of barriers—technological and political.

### Technological Barriers

A discussion of the technological barriers to NBC terrorism must take into account the fact that while virtually any NBC terrorism could produce greater effects than the traditional conventional explosives historically preferred by terrorist groups, this increased effectiveness may not be desired and would not come without some costs. For most terrorist groups, it would appear that the simpler, less expensive, and more predictable results of conventional explosives are the favored means to achieve the desired ends. The discussion must also recognize that the global diffusion of key technologies is gradually eroding those barriers. However, barriers do remain at present and are very different for the different NBC arenas.

**Nuclear.** There are substantial technological barriers to the fabrication and use of nuclear weapons. Nuclear terrorism utilizing weapons-grade materials—highly enriched uranium or plutonium—would appear to confront the terrorists with extremely difficult technological tasks. Theft or diversion of enough weapons-grade material to make nuclear explosives would require extensive resources, although they could conceivably be obtained. One of the new pathways to terrorists' obtaining nuclear materials is nuclear smuggling, but the smuggling threat, while new, may not be as extensive as is sometimes claimed. Moreover, most of the reports of smuggling, with some notable exceptions, do not involve weapons-usable materials. In any event, nuclear material could be diverted by successful infiltration of a nuclear facility, or obtained by theft from such facilities or during transport. Handling the material would pose certain technical and safety problems, which would depend on the material itself, its quantity, form, and the manner in which it is packaged.

If the terrorists' objective were to disperse radioactive material, the technical requirements could range from the relatively rudimentary to the sophisticated, depending on the effect sought and other factors. If they intend to fabricate a nuclear explosive device, however, the technical requirements increase significantly. The technological expertise required to fabricate a crude explosive device has been the subject of controversy since the mid-1970s. Early concerns that a few individuals could construct a low-yield nuclear explosive device are still expressed, but they may be exaggerated. In any event, no such device is known to have been built or tested by terrorists. And the prevailing view among experts appears to be that fabrication of a bomb, even with high-grade, weapons-grade material, would be extremely difficult, but not impossible, for a well-organized, well-financed terrorist group. In this vein, according to Thomas Schelling, "... it appears to require a group of significant size, high professional quality, and excellent organization and discipline to convert unauthorized or illicitly obtained nuclear materials into a usable weapon."[8]

**Biological.** The production of biological agents can be undertaken in a small facility, with no distinguishing features or signatures. Currently, cultures can be readily obtained from commercial houses or even from nature. Aum Shinrikyo reportedly sent members on a medical mission to Zaire during an outbreak of the Ebola virus in 1992, presumably in the hopes of obtaining a sample of the deadly virus.[9] Only relatively small quantities of agent are required. Advances in biotechnology could increase the potency or survivability of the agent or toxin, or lead to the creation of entirely new organisms. These advanced technologies would be more difficult to achieve by terrorists or subnational groups, but lower technology options abound. Biological agents and toxins can be dispersed in the air or in water, but their dispersion and survivability are factors that must be taken into account in ensuring effective dissemination. The problem of the deterioration of the agents prior to and during dissemination is critical in this respect. Although exotic pathogens and sophisticated dispersal methods would provide challenges to terrorists, the production and dispersal of agents such as anthrax would probably not pose challenges that a modestly funded terrorist group with some technical expertise and specialized scientific knowledge could not meet. The greatest technical barriers may be the unpredictability of the effect and the presence of a lag time of from hours to weeks before any significant effects appear.

**Chemical.** Chemical agents can be synthesized in laboratories or in production plants with relative ease even under suboptimal conditions. Aum Shinrikyo developed the capability to produce sarin, tabun, soman, and VX at a sophisticated facility of their own, staffed by educated and trained personnel. Small quantities of sarin were produced and used in the subway attack in Tokyo and in an earlier attack in Matsumoto.

Members of the sect have been charged with planning to produce 70 tons of sarin within 40 days after the completion of a production facility. The knowledge of chemical weapon production is widespread, and knowledge on sarin production is available on the Internet from "Uncle Fester" and other sources. Such simple agents as chlorine and mustard gas are readily available and even easier to synthesize. In both cases, precursor chemicals currently are widely available, as evidenced by Aum's ability to acquire them without arousing attention, despite existing controls. Effective weaponization or dissemination is more challenging because environmental conditions could greatly influence the effectiveness of CW, but in some respects dissemination inefficiencies can be overcome by producing and disseminating large quantities of the agent. The technical barriers for CW production and dissemination are low and within the reach of subnational groups and terrorist organizations. Weaponization is more problematic but may not be a requirement for these groups.

## POLITICAL CONSIDERATIONS

Along with technological barriers, political considerations appear to have constrained terrorists from acts of mass destruction using nuclear materials or weapons. Actions that are less difficult to undertake and cause less destruction are more likely to be attempted if they are believed to be effective in attaining the terrorists' ends. Although terrorists have often been labeled as indiscriminate mass murderers, without moral and political restraint, who have no territories or populations to protect, this image is simplistic and, because it does not reflect the heterogeneity of terrorist organizations, it is misleading.

Regarding political and organizational restraints that might limit the violence of the terrorists, it is important to note that many contemporary terrorist organizations regard themselves as alternative governments. From this perspective, unjustifiable or indiscriminate killing might be seen by the terrorists themselves as jeopardizing perceptions of their legitimacy.[10]

With the exception of Aum Shinrikyo, terrorists may not have engaged in NBC terrorism because there was little or no advantage to them from such an act. Mass destruction has not been an objective in itself, and this may even hold for the Aum sect.[11] Japanese authorities reportedly believe that the Tokyo attack constituted a test and that the real objective of Aum Shinrikyo was to overthrow the government and the military (although this may have entailed the use of large-scale chemical weapons). In any event, indiscriminate threats involving nuclear weapons have not often been made by terrorist groups. While terrorists may recognize the tremendous coercive power they might derive from the possession of a nuclear weapon, or other weapons of mass destruction, they may also recognize the high political risks of making NBC threats.[12]

What are the political risks? What negative reactions might terrorists expect to follow their use of NBC material or weapons to cause mass casualties? Murder on a massive scale could be expected to provoke widespread world revulsion, erode support among sympathizers, cause severe governmental reactions, provoke retaliation against the domestic or international supporters of the terrorists and their bases of operation, and, finally, divide the group and open it to betrayal.[13] Historically, the terrorist organizations most likely to have the resources, technical expertise, and command and control capability that could allow them to undertake acts of NBC terrorism are precisely those organizations that will most seriously weigh these political factors and could, under most circumstances, be expected to be deterred by them.[14] The case of Aum, however, is not so clear from this perspective. Considerable resources and technical expertise were available to Aum, but the attack also shows a level of ineptitude not unlike what we have witnessed in the past, even though it was more deadly than prior abortive incidents using nuclear, chemical, or biological materials.

On a related issue, experts previously believed that terrorists acting across national boundaries would be more likely to engage in mass destruction terrorism than terrorists operating within their own country. In the latter case, such an act would be counterproductive in most circumstances. Nevertheless, Aum's actions again provide a case where the behavior differs from the predictions of experts, because they did not account for what was an unprecedented aspect of the Aum attack, that is, an apocalyptic group directly targeting its own country.

Aside from these technological and political barriers, it is difficult to develop credible scenarios for terrorists' undertaking significant acts of NBC terrorism. What would be their demands? How could they assure a state or states that submitting to their demands would end the threat? What are the prospects of a state or states submitting to NBC extortion? What level of casualties would a terrorist organization be willing to cause? Could this ever be acceptable to a threatened state? What alternatives would the state have? According to one expert addressing nuclear terrorism:

> ...if terrorists had a nuclear capability, they would be more likely to brandish it as a threat than detonate it, although one can scarcely conceive of a more emotional use of a nuclear weapon by a desperate group than as the ultimate instrument of revenge or as a "Doomsday Machine." Translating the enormous coercive power of a nuclear weapon into concrete political gains, however, would pose some difficulty for terrorists. First, they would have to establish the credibility of the threat....Second, the terrorists would have to persuade the government that it has an incentive to negotiate.... we may assume that the terrorists' demands would be commensurate with the magnitude of the threat. Governments facing the threat of nuclear terrorism would paradoxically find it more difficult to refuse, yet more difficult to yield. Impossible demands—for example, that a government liquidate itself—could not be met under a nuclear threat. Nor could terrorists enforce permanent policy changes unless they maintained the threat indefinitely. And if a government could not be assured that the threat would be dismantled once the demands were met, it would have little incentive to negotiate....[15]

He continued, however, to suggest that we could possibly see finite, irrevocable demands put forward by terrorists. If governments could meet those demands, and receive adequate assurances that meeting those demands would bring an end to the threats, their calculations may differ from those presented above.[16] Although this notion is, in principle, valid, it is difficult to imagine what such demands might be. Demands that a government abolish itself or key agencies or individuals within it would not be seen as finite or irrevocable. It seems unlikely that terrorists would threaten nuclear terrorism to obtain the release of their imprisoned comrades or for some similar objective. If terrorists did threaten nuclear terrorism for political gain or extortion, it would probably be seen as dangerous and intolerable and could not be disregarded by the United States and the international community. Similar calculations would seem to apply to biological weapons and, possibly, to chemical weapons.

## WILL NBC TERRORISM BE UNDERTAKEN IN THE FUTURE?

If there have been technological and political reasons why the full range of possibilities associated with NBC terrorism has not been realized, there are conditions in which they could occur in the future. These conditions involve the erosion of the political and technical barriers that terrorists have confronted in the past, but the erosion of those barriers, even if they make NBC terrorism more likely, would not make it inevitable.

Currently, the greatest fears of analysts examining the potential for NBC terrorism are based on the belief that an increase in the technical capabilities of the terrorists, or greater access to weapons or a significant quantity of agent or nuclear material, could reduce technological barriers and make NBC terrorism more appealing. However, this view equates "opportunities" with their realization and assumes that technical barriers have been the primary reason terrorists have not engaged in serious NBC terrorism. This does not appear to have been the principal driver behind the absence of significant NBC terrorism in the past, although the increasing accessibility of NBC capabilities will be important in the future.

The erosion of political barriers is potentially more significant.[17] In the future, terrorists may be driven to more extreme acts by the erosion of popular support for, or interest in, their actions; by a decline in their ability, whether real or perceived, to obtain publicity or to coerce governments; or by the self-perception of the terrorists that they face defeat unless they resort to extreme measures. The propensity to consider mass destruction may also be driven by the growing callousness, even brutalization of terrorists after years of violent struggle; by a change in the composition of groups as they attract those with a psychological predisposition to violence; or by a growth in extreme terrorism following initial successful use of indiscriminate massacres by terrorists. Because of the terrorists' quest for public drama, NBC terrorism could be engendered by the increased public attention to—and thus fear of—NBC weapons technologies and even NBC-related commercial activities, such as nuclear power generation and genetic research. Emerging terrorist groups already reveal elements of such extremism, which makes NBC terrorism more likely in the future.

Finally, there is a concern based on political and technological calculations that NBC terrorism—or at least some of its possibilities—is more likely under state sponsorship.[18] State sponsorship can, in principle, provide terrorists with more resources than they would otherwise have, particularly funding, intelligence, sophisticated weaponry, and technical expertise. It can also remove certain constraints on the terrorists' actions, perhaps by giving them hopes of protection in the belief that they were serving a higher cause, which could result in increasing the level of violence of terrorist operations.

Nonetheless, this by no means indicates that state-sponsored NBC terrorism is likely in the near term. What might a state hope to gain? A state might believe that using terrorists would allow it to threaten or use weapons of mass run destruction without the risk of direct retaliation. But it is not clear that this belief would be compelling. Would a country sponsoring NBC terrorism be willing to risk possible retaliation? Could it control terrorist clients once they had possession of an NBC weapon, especially a nuclear weapon? Could it hope to maintain deniability? Would the victim of an NBC terrorist attack strike back if there were uncertainty about the origins of the attack? Under unbearable pressures to react, what levels of certitude about the perpetrators of such an attack would be required?

On the basis of such considerations, it seems highly unlikely that states would offer support for acts of NBC terrorism. Even unstable regimes known to support terrorism would most likely resist providing NBC weapons to terrorist groups or would deny sanctuary to terrorists who had succeeded in stealing agents or nuclear materials or stealing or fabricating a weapon or device. States might also conclude that NBC weapons provided to terrorists might constitute an unacceptable danger to themselves or their allies. These states might also fear that any support they might provide, if it became known, would result in intense political pressures and the possibility of large-scale military action directed against them.

# ASSESSING DOMESTIC VULNERABILITIES

However NBC terrorism may play out in the future, it is clear that the United States and other democracies are vulnerable to NBC attacks and to other forms of terrorism. Vulnerabilities must be addressed on the basis of sober analysis and the prioritization of risks. NBC attacks on the Capitol, the White House, the Pentagon, or other functioning or symbolic buildings are the basis of most scenarios generated in governmental and academic circles. Attacks on the U.S. populace in subways and large office complexes are also considered. Prior to Aum Shinrikyo's gassing of a crowded Tokyo subway, however, these scenarios were purely speculative. The subway attack changed the picture by making it impossible to dismiss the likelihood of such attacks out of hand. Nonetheless, the Tokyo attack has resulted in overreaction by many commentators, a hyping of the policy agenda, and a tendency to see weaknesses everywhere. Civilian vulnerabilities—particularity the vulnerability of the American people and U.S. economic interests—are at the forefront of political concern. If an attack occurs, especially if nothing has been done by the government to prevent it, the very fabric of American politics and society could change.

These concerns are real, and need to be addressed. Civilian vulnerability to NBC terrorism has not been systematically addressed; the focus has been on NBC threats to military forces. Now that the political concerns about NBC terrorism are centered on the threat to the United States, the issue of domestic vulnerability has been highlighted and exacerbated by the attention of analysts and others eager to point out every horrible possibility. Protection of the U.S. population and assets is a difficult problem. Civilian crisis management organizations do not now have the experience, resources, or political leverage to effectively respond to NBC terrorism, and the military continues to have misgivings about getting involved in this mission.

Even if these problems are resolved, basing a response on all possible vulnerabilities is likely to be counterproductive and could create public concerns without of addressing them adequately. It is critical to address systematically certain vulnerabilities to NBC attacks, in order to defend against both complacency and panic. To do so is an enormous task, with sensitive political issues like civil defense and civil rights that require attention, along with technical issues such as modeling the effects of a low-yield nuclear blast in a large city or understanding the dispersal of chemical or biological agents in a high-rise building or a busy metropolitan intersection. Given the magnitude of the effort required, it would be sensible to begin with the experience in Tokyo, recalling that the death total there—however tragic—fell within the loss of life typically associated with conventional terrorism. What could have been done to prevent this tragic event? Clearly, the principles of democratic societies set significant limits on preventive actions. But adequate intelligence, surveillance, and intervention by the Japanese authorities was certainly possible, and might well have been effective. The next section will explore some of these issues.

## Responding to NBC Terrorism

Although vulnerabilities cannot be totally removed in democracies, effective counterterrorism strategies can be undertaken. In consider-

ing responses, it will be necessary to seek to prevent, neutr
mitigate the most likely kinds of attacks. In the current politi
budgetary climate, it will not be possible to start and sustain a program
based on worst-case scenarios that are incredible. Strategically, NBC
terrorism must be countered using the same approaches as conventional terrorism. However, some special tools, especially those involving enhanced technologies, may be appropriate and necessary. Specifically, intelligence and threat assessment are the most important tools
in combating NBC terrorism, but protection at the source for nuclear
materials and NBC weapons, export controls and monitoring, and various detection, interdiction, forensic, and mediation tools are critical to
the fight. Protective measures in high-risk areas may also be effective;
more general civil defense preparedness is important and potentially
effective in principle, but problematic. It is not clear that resources will
be devoted to this task or how accepted or applied such efforts would
be in the end. Let us address each of these areas in more detail, focusing on their unique technological challenges.

Intelligence has been at the forefront of counterterrorism efforts,
and it will have that role in combating NBC terrorism. Good intelligence is central to the difficult issue of threat assessment and characterization, and it can provide early warning of terrorist attacks or their
preparations for developing NBC attacks. In addition to focusing intelligence resources on this problem, the priorities of monitoring, detecting, collecting, and integrating information relating to theft or diversion of agents, materials, and equipment need to be addressed through
improved tools.

Detection and monitoring, enhanced by technology, can be important tools of intelligence, in the best cases providing early warning of a
diversion or theft of materials or of an attack that allows preemption or
interdiction. There are requirements for portable, fieldable instrumentation and for sensitive NBC sensors for use in satellite-based monitoring, unattended ground sensors, and other applications. Increasing the
sensitivity, selectivity, and effective range of sensors and other improvements is desirable and potentially critical. Field prototyping and operational support are needs that will ensure the utility of improved

sensor and related capabilities. Information management—the enhanced ability to fuse together enormous amounts of diverse data from different types of sensors—is needed for the task of providing usable intelligence to those in the field.

There is a high value to protecting agents, materials, and equipment and technologies at the source, a problem related to international nonproliferation regimes for dealing with nuclear, biological, and chemical weapons. The safeguards of the Nuclear Non-Proliferation Treaty (NPT) and other such activities (e.g., those under the rubric of Materials Protection, Control, and Accounting, or MPC&A) are critical for securing nuclear materials at the source. In response to nuclear smuggling, threat characterization (forensics and attribution analysis), improved MPC&A, containment and surveillance, portal monitoring, tracking nuclear materials in transport, and response efforts have been identified as useful. Similar approaches may be less germane in the chemical and biological areas. In this context, it should be noted that the Biological and Toxin Weapons Convention (BWC) currently has no verification regime, and there are only limited prospects of achieving an effective verification regime for the BWC at a reasonable cost.

In the same manner, export controls offer means of limiting access to nuclear-related equipment and materials and to chemical and biological agents, but they are not central to preventing NBC terrorism. Existing international regimes and arrangements currently operate in the NBC arena, and if the Chemical Weapons Convention (CWC) enters into force, it will require parties to enact national legislation that will contribute to controlling chemical agents and technologies. However, all export-control regimes have difficulty in dealing with dual-use materials, and this problem is more significant for chemical and biological agents and equipment than for nuclear materials and related technologies. Denying access to NBC-related exports can inhibit legitimate commercial interests and cannot, therefore, be a tool used indiscriminately or profligately. However effective or ineffective for that purpose, monitoring sales, transfers, and other transactions of nuclear equipment, precursor chemicals, chemical process equipment, and biological feed material can provide information of value for intelligence and threat assessments and should be effectively used by intelligence processing and analysis systems. Tags or markers can be used to track nuclear and other materials and provide information necessary for identification and attribution of the agent or material used in an attack as well as for protection and mitigation.

Finally, because not all attacks can be prevented, technology-enhanced responses are necessary. The Nuclear Emergency Search Team (NEST) is an existing instrument for responding to nuclear terrorist threats and incidents, with capabilities to assess, defeat, disable, and dismantle nuclear devices and to mitigate the effects of such devices. The Accident Response Group (ARG) is also capable of responding to nuclear terrorism and has been working with the Russians on weapon safety and security issues, including nuclear weapon security during transport. Interdiction, crisis management, and emergency response require forensics and attribution analysis, protection technologies, and neutralization, mitigation, and decontamination technologies.

## CONCLUSIONS

The prospects for NBC terrorism have been exaggerated since the Tokyo tragedy. Such terrorism is possible, but not probable, given the interests and objectives of most terrorist groups with which we are familiar or that may appear on the horizon. The capabilities that NBC terrorism would require and the difficulties and dangers it would present to the terrorists are also factors suggesting it is not probable. If mass-destruction terrorism were to occur, it would more likely be chemical or biological than nuclear, with chemical terrorism perhaps the most likely prospect of all.

The likelihood that a terrorist group could successfully combine the material resources, technical skills, and motivations necessary to perpetrate an act resulting in mass destruction remains low, but the results could have the highest level of consequences for society. Casualties and damage produced might be several orders of magnitude greater than any terrorist attack of the past. Moreover, as we have suggested, the probability of an attack could increase over time, especially as technical barriers to such terrorism continue to erode.

Despite real uncertainties about the future of NBC terrorism—some of which are intrinsic to projections on terrorism and some specific to this new, largely uncharacterized phenomenon—it has potentially such great consequences that it will be important to understand better the parameters of the phenomenon and monitor groups and activities identified with mass destruction terrorism. It will also be important to prioritize the more likely attacks, for terrorists may be unwilling or unable to fully exploit NBC weapons and materials. On this basis, the analysis of key issues ranging from the prevention of NBC acquisition and use to protection during and cleanup after an attack needs to begin immediately. What are the NBC threats that should be taken into account in military and civil planning processes? What approaches might be considered to deny access to potential threats (e.g., centralizing and protecting agents and materials in use and storage)? What are the prospects of success for denial-based approaches? What are the intelligence requirements for effectively countering NBC proliferation and terrorism? Can these requirements be met now or in the future? How should we create new intelligence capabilities to meet emerging threats? Are improvements in collection, analysis, and distribution needed and are they possible?

In terms of response planning, what capabilities and approaches might be applicable to NBC terrorism? What national and international mechanisms currently exist to respond to NBC incidents? Will these mechanisms be useful for responding to the emerging threat? What deficiencies can be identified? What approaches hold out promise to improve the situation? How critical is widespread civil defense? What new military roles could emerge? What technical means might be used to neutralize or interdict weapons or materials? What are the technical challenges we might confront? What operational challenges or obstacles can be expected? What are the key problems that will be encountered after an NBC attack, and how might they be solved?

Such analytic requirements will not be easily undertaken and completed, but they must be taken seriously. The stakes are too high to do otherwise.

# NOTES

1. John Deutch, "Worldwide Threat Assessment Brief to the Senate Select Committee on Intelligence," Statement for the Record, February 22, 1996, pp. 16-18.

2. Notably, the U.S. Senate Permanent Subcommittee on Investigations, Committee on Governmental Affairs, held hearings on The Global Proliferation of Weapons of Mass Destruction, March 13, 20, 27, 1996. NBC terrorism figured prominently in the hearings.

3. Brian Jenkins, "Nuclear Terrorism and Its Consequences," *Society/Social Science and Modern Society*, vol. 17 (July/August 1980), p. 6.

4. Ibid., p. 7.

5. Deutch, "Worldwide Threat Assessment Brief," p. 16.

6. Ibid.

7. Ibid.

8. Thomas Schelling, "Thinking About Nuclear Terrorism," *International Security*, vol. 6, no. 4 (Spring 1982), p. 65.

9. See Minority Staff Statement, U.S. Senate Permanent Subcommittee on Investigations, Committee on Governmental Affairs, "Hearings on Global Proliferation of Weapons of Mass Destruction: A Case Study of Aum Shinrikyo", October 31, 1995, p. 44.

10. Jenkins, "Terrorism in the 1980s," RAND Paper P6564 (Santa Monica, CA: RAND, December 1980), p. 6.

11. Ibid., p. 7.

12. See, for example, ibid., p. 6.

13. Ibid.

14. Ibid., p. 7.

15. Jenkins, "Will Terrorists Go Nuclear?" *Orbis*, vol. 29, no. 3 (Fall 1985), pp. 514-515.

16. Ibid., p. 515.

17. See Jenkins, "Terrorism in the 1980s," p. 7.

18. See, for example, Konrad Kellen, "The Potential for Nuclear Terrorism: A Discussion," in *Preventing Nuclear Terrorism: The Report and Papers of the International Task Force on Prevention of Nuclear Terrorism*, Paul Leventhal and Yonah Alexander, eds. (Lexington, MA, and Toronto: Lexington Books, D.C. Heath and Company, 1987), p. 118; and Eugene Mastrangelo, "Terrorist Activities by Region," in *Preventing Nuclear Terrorism*, pp. 141-142.

# The Dangerous New World of Chemical and Biological Weapons

## James Adams

In 1993, South Africa signed the Chemical Weapons Convention (CWC) as part of its efforts to gain acceptance by the international community after the end of apartheid and the establishment of a democratic government. By signing the convention, the government abandoned one of the best kept secrets of the apartheid era: a huge and successful chemical and biological weapons (CBW) program.

Known as Project B or Project Coast, the CBW program was controlled by the South African Ministry of Defense using two principal front companies, Roodeplaay Research Laboratories and Delta G.[1] While Western intelligence had known of the existence of the chemical weapons (CW) program, the fact that South Africa had successfully produced biological weapons was not known until three years ago.

During the 1980s, the South African government used its CBW capability in various ways. Chemical weapons were used in Namibia and Angola as well as against very specific targets of assassination and as part of wide-ranging psychological operations, including impregnating the clothing of anti-apartheid activists and using poisons to kill opponents abroad. In addition, the government is believed to have developed a new and exceptionally virulent strain of malaria, which was deployed in Angola, and used anthrax on behalf of the Rhodesian government in their fight against guerrillas fighting for the independence of that country.[2]

The fact that South Africa signed the Chemical Weapons Convention was naturally welcomed by the Clinton administration. As a signatory, the South Africans were obliged to shut down their chemical weapons program and destroy the stocks that had been stored over the previous decade. On the personal instructions of President Nelson Mandela this began to be carried out and is ongoing.

The future of the South African biological weapons (BW) program was less clear. BW are not covered by the CWC and compliance is much more difficult to police. There are not necessarily any large factories to inspect and it is difficult to check on the status of the intellectual property that has been generated in the course of developing the BW capability.

During 1993 and early 1994, the British and American governments held a series of meetings with senior officials in the South African government to press for the destruction of all research material relating to the BW program. President Mandela gave his personal assurance that this would be done. However, the South African defense force refused to carry out his instructions.[3]

## THE LIBYAN CASE

Then, in the late summer of 1994, Western intelligence received reliable information that the Libyan government was attempting to recruit scientists from the South African BW project to come to Tripoli to establish a similar program for Colonel Mu'ammer Qadhafi. The Central Intelligence Agency (CIA) and Britain's Secret Intelligence Service (SIS) mounted a large intelligence operation which was designed to thwart this effort and as part of that operation, both the British and U.S. governments increased the political pressure on President Mandela.

This was an entirely covert effort with no discussion either of South Africa's BW program or of efforts to shut it down, or of Qadhafi's attempts to buy his own program. Part of the reason for this was that there was considerable nervousness in the Clinton administration that open discussion of the problem, which might have shut down the Libyan part of the operation, might also have done considerable damage to Mandela, who would have been exposed as a weak leader with limited authority over his country's armed forces.

The result of the private pressure was a stalemate. President Mandela could do nothing, U.S. and British pressure was apparently worthless, and the South African military felt no compelling reason to destroy the research they had worked so hard to perfect. Meanwhile, Qadhafi's agents had successfully lured a South African scientist to Tripoli on an all-expenses-paid vacation and believed that with a little more persuasion he would leave South Africa permanently.

In the event, a decision was made to leak the details about Libya's efforts to acquire BW to the press and a front page article appeared in the London *Sunday Times* on February 26, 1995. The revelations provoked a political storm in South Africa and successfully stopped the Libyan procurement effort. More than a year later, Qadhafi's efforts to acquire biological weapons have not resumed.

It would be easy to use that single example as an illustration of a changed world since the end of the Cold War. After all, it does illustrate that the changed international order has produced different alliances and altered pressure points. Some would argue that the end of the superpower struggle between the Soviet Union and the United States has actually made management of the CBW environment infinitely more difficult. During the Cold War, both superpowers were able to control their allies and those allies had every reason (money, arms, trade, diplomatic support) to abide their wishes. The end of that struggle has freed many of the old constraints and produced a worldwide security environment where pressure points are fewer and controls are less or have vanished altogether.

In the case of the Libyan BW effort, Colonel Qadhafi was able to develop a relationship with the South African government that would have been unthinkable in the apartheid era. At the same time, the Clinton administration was limited by political sensitivities about just how much could be done to control the government of President Mandela. It was also a clear illustration of the limitations of intelligence in this new world. As happens all too infrequently, there was very good and reliable intelligence that provided details of the Libyan procurement effort. These details were unambiguous and sufficient for the policy makers to use for action but for the reasons outlined above, the pressure applied was insufficient.

# THE PROBLEM OF
# POROUS BORDERS

For the intelligence community, there is now recognition that the current international climate makes counterproliferation in the CBW area—preventing the spread of these weapons from country to country and country to group—an impossible task that will never be fully accomplished. There are too many porous borders, too many weak governments, and a lack of aggressive political will that means that even the best intelligence is often not enough to prevent proliferation.

One of the best examples of this is, once again, Libya. In 1985, the West German firm Imhausen-Chemis drew up plans for a chemical weapons plant to be built at Rabta in Libya. Some work on the project was carried out by Salzgitter Steel Company, which is owned by the German government, who believed that the designs were for a pharmaceutical complex in Hong Kong. The Japan Steel Works did much of the construction work at Rabta using Thai workers and by 1988 the plant was producing nerve-gas casings using steel supplied by other German companies.[4] Western intelligence had been keeping a close eye on the project and were certain that it would soon become the largest chemical weapons plant in the Third World, capable of producing up to 84,000 pounds of nerve agents every day.

The Bush administration decided on a policy of aggressive confrontation. When the Japanese government was approached about its involvement, they claimed the project was a desalination plant, even though Rabta is 50 miles from the sea. The Thais and the Germans were just as obstructive and, of course, there was little that could be done to pressure the Libyans, who were already suffering from international sanctions. Once again, publicity that exposed the plant helped shut the project down. Foreign workers were scared away from completing the project and the Libyans were unable to maintain the sensitive equipment, which rusted and then was largely destroyed in a mysterious fire.

But even before Rabta had ground to a halt, Qadhafi had begun construction on a second, less vulnerable, plant at Tarhuna, 40 miles southeast of Tripoli. The designs for the plant, which have been obtained by Western intelligence, call for two huge tunnels, each 450 feet long and 40 feet wide and connected by a series of smaller cross tunnels. One tunnel houses the production facility and the second is a storage area for the chemical weapons. Both have been hardened to withstand bombs and missiles. A direct attack at the main entrance is also impossible. The tunnels lie at the end of a valley inside a mountain range and the valley itself has a dog leg which makes it impossible for an aircraft to fly a low level attack successfully.[5]

Qadhafi announced that the massive engineering required at Tarhuna was all part of the Man Made River irrigation project which was an ambitious scheme to "make the desert bloom." To reduce his dependence on overseas sources, Qadhafi also decided to produce many of the chemical precursors himself. To that end, he announced that he would build a new petrochemical plant to produce lubricants and solvents. Many of those products require the same raw materials as chemical weapons and the Libyans hoped that it would be impossible for the Western intelligence agencies watching the Tarhuna project to distinguish between the legitimate and the illegitimate.

For the past six years there has been an aggressive intelligence operation mounted against the Libyans, which has been led by the CIA with some assistance from other friendly intelligence services. The Libyan procurement network has been quite extensively penetrated and it has been possible to build up a very detailed knowledge of the plant, the raw materials ordered, and the progress that has been made on the project. But even with that knowledge, it has proved impossible to stop the project. It has been possible, however, to use the available intelligence to thwart some parts of Qadhafi's plans and so delay the project which is now running three years behind schedule.

For example, in February 1993, Western intelligence picked up some information from a source in Malaysia that the Libyans had ordered a consignment of eight stainless steel canisters to store a mud-like solution used for lubricating drill bits used in oil exploration. Superficially, this was just another contract for Qadhafi's new petrochemical plant but the specifications for the canisters were far more precise than those needed for a petrochemical project and were precisely those required for mixing the highly corrosive ingredients for nerve gas. The Libyans also placed an order for 60 tons of ammonium perchlorate, a chemical ingredient for rocket fuel, which the Libyans need for their ballistic missile development program.

Both contractors were contacted but neither was prepared to cancel the deal, claiming that the order was for civilian purposes and thus fell outside the United Nations sanctions regime designed to control the transfer of military-related material. But the goods were to be shipped from Russia via the Ukraine and from Malaysia via Singapore and so there would be a second opportunity to apply pressure. Eventually, both shipments were seized and Qadhafi had to look elsewhere for his raw material.

There followed a dance through the seedier ports of the world with U.S. and British intelligence agents trying to track every shipment destined for Libya's chemical plant. One particular order was placed in five different countries and intercepted in each one, a process that took nearly two years. A sixth shipment from an unknown supplier eventually got through.

Workers for the Tarhuna project were supplied by two Thai companies as part of a generous Libyan deal that called for thousands of foreign workers, mostly from Thailand, to carry out the more mundane construction tasks in the country. For two years starting in 1992, the Clinton administration attempted to force the cancellation of the labor contracts by pressuring the Thai government to take action. It took a personal plea from Warren Christopher, the U.S. secretary of state, to Prasong Sunsiri, the Thai foreign minister, before a commitment was made to stop the flow of workers to the project. In any case, the promises proved worthless and Thai workers are busy completing the project. Such competing interests typically face governments when confronted with problems of proliferation. For the Thais, the Libyan contract was worth a great deal of money in its own right. In addition, Thais form a large proportion of the expatriate workers in Libya and are a valuable source of foreign exchange for the Thai government and a useful contributor to the Thai economy. The same applies to Germany's relationship with Libya, which is long standing and involves extensive trading links. When the United States or any other third party tries to break those existing relationships with intelligence information that is often fragmentary and almost always promises future dangers rather than current risk, it is all too easy for the country under pressure to refuse to act. It is rare indeed that the United States or any other country will rush to offer compensation for lost trade and income. Instead, countries are supposed to respond to moral arguments that are usually not strong enough on their own to do the job.

At the beginning of 1996, it was clear that if the Libyans continued at their current rate of progress, the six-acre chemical plant would be fully operational by the end of the decade and there was nothing that the best efforts of the intelligence community would be able to do about it. In a review of the options ordered by William Perry, the U.S. secretary of defense, the Pentagon concluded that a direct air attack would fail, as would an assault by special forces.[6]

In April, the United States was a signatory to an international agreement that made Africa a nuclear free zone. However, the wording of the agreement was framed in such a way as to allow the United States to use nuclear weapons under certain special circumstances. One circumstance envisaged was a nuclear strike on the Libyan plant at Tarhuna.

Recognition of the political fallout from such an action led the administration to launch an aggressive publicity campaign designed to intimidate Qadhafi into closing down the plant. There was some hope that as a similar effort had worked at Rabta, it might work again at Tarhuna. Psychologists had ample evidence that Qadhafi is vulnerable to that kind of pressure and takes seriously direct threats he believes could affect him personally.

To emphasize the United States' determination to stop the plant, Secretary of Defense Perry flew to Cairo for talks with President Mubarak of Egypt in April. Perry supplied detailed intelligence, including satellite photographs, to Mubarak who promised to use what influence he had with Qadhafi to get the project stopped.[7] Mubarak and Qadhafi met in May and according to the Egyptian leader he was given an understanding that the plant would not be used to make chemical weapons. Although work on the outside of the plant had ceased by the middle of June, there remains considerable uncertainty within Western intelligence about whether work continues inside the mountain, out of sight of prying satellites.[8]

# THE IMPACT OF
# SOVIET COLLAPSE

It can be argued that Libya's pursuit of chemical weapons would have happened with or without the collapse of communism. Indeed, construction began on the Rabta plant while the Soviet Union still existed and Tarhuna was conceived by Qadhafi in the midst of the Gorbachev revolution. The intelligence community argues that it is the very loosening of Cold War bipolar structures that has allowed Qadhafi to pursue his CBW ambitions. Without that loosing of constraints, he would have found it more difficult, if not impossible, to acquire either BW or CW capability.

Those loosened constraints have been caused primarily by the collapse of the Soviet Union. Instead of a single superpower controlling its global empire, disintegration of central control has led to an almost total breakdown of influence externally. For decades, what Moscow wanted, client states faithfully executed; what Moscow did not want, it was able to prevent without subsidies and favored trading status. Client relationships had disadvantages when, for example, the Soviet Union was interested in using terrorism as a political weapon. But there were also significant advantages as the Soviets did much to control the proliferation of nuclear weapons and other weapons of mass destruction.

In theory, the establishment of democracy in Russia should have brought about a more transparent and cooperative government and meaningful public oversight. The reverse has happened. With the loosening of the central controls inherent in a communist regime, organized crime has flourished in a fashion unprecedented in the modern world. With the assistance of current and former members of Soviet intelligence, organized criminals have penetrated every aspect of Russian society and have exploited every opportunity to make money out of the remnants of the old Soviet system. Nowhere has this been more apparent than in the field of chemical and biological weapons.

The Soviet regime believed that CBW were an essential part of the military structure. NATO recognized that the Soviets had the largest chemical arsenal in the world and knew, too, that Soviet doctrine required the use of such weapons in any conventional confrontation. What was not known for much of the Cold War was the emphasis that the Soviets placed on biological weapons as well.

## THE SOVIET BW PROGRAM

Beginning in the early 1970s, the Main Board of the Microbiological Industry, working under the auspices of the Soviet Ministry of Defense, set up a nationwide research program called Biopreparat. The project was supposed to be carrying out medical and biological research on cures for cancer and crop protection. In fact, it was the largest investment in perfecting new forms of biological weapons ever known. Biopreparat was responsible for overseeing two institutes in Moscow itself, two in the Serpukhov region on the edge of the capital (Obolensk and Chekhov), one in Noveosibirsk (Koltsovo), one in Leningrad and manufacturing plants at Omutninsk, Stepnogorsk, Berdsk, Kirishi and Yoshkar-Ola. The plants employed a total of 15,000 men and women, and later included on the staff several members of the Soviet Academy of Sciences.[9] The scale of this investment that eventually cost hundreds of millions of dollars illustrates clearly just how difficult the manufacture of BW is—provided it is intended for use on the battlefield against military and civilian targets as part of a coherent strategy. The Soviets discovered that they confronted two principal difficulties: making strains of BW that were non-persistent, that is, that would survive a specified time and allow conquering troops to enter a territory without fear of being infected; and finding a method to deliver the virus that would ensure coverage over specific areas.

It was not until 1981 that the research laboratories began engineering new biological weapons that could be suspended as an aerosol. The problem for the Biopreparat scientists was to develop new strains of known diseases that would be far more powerful than anything known to science. Two of these weapons were based on a form of pneumonic plague and of tularemia. The scientists were required to ensure that these new strains could be delivered by artillery shell, bomb, or missile and have a long enough life in the open air to infect a large enough area to make them militarily effective. The strains had to be resistant to known antibodies available to NATO armies.

In 1983, with the help of the technological work at the institute in Leningrad, the All Union Research Institute of Applied Microbiology at Obolensk, 60 miles south of Moscow, developed a new strain of the tularemia agent. The new weapon was a dry powder, a form of superplague, and the tests were sufficiently encouraging for Moscow to give the go-ahead for full scale development and production of the agent.

In 1985, Biopreparat's new Five Year Plan called for the institute at Obolensk to develop an even more deadly agent based on a strain of pneumonic plague. After two years of the five year plan, the Soviets had sufficient industrial capacity to manufacture 200 kilograms per week of the superplague agent, which would be enough to kill 500,00 people for each week of production.

Senior Soviet generals in the 15th Directorate of the Ministry of Defense in charge of the Biological Warfare program understood the value of these new weapons and they were quickly accepted into service. Known as the Weapons of Special Designation, they would be used, not only as a weapon of last resort, but as a tool in support of a conventional conflict to attack troop reserves and to hamper logistical operations at ports and rail centers.

As the superplague had a short life, there was no manufacture of the agents except for testing. Instead, the Biopreparat network was instructed to be ready to begin full scale production at a time designated Day X. Meanwhile, other institutes in Biopreparat were involved in research into other genetically engineered weapons with similar results.

Every part of this program was in breach of the 1972 Biological and Toxin Weapons Convention which the Soviets had signed. Aside from being in breach of international agreements, the whole of the offensive biological warfare activity of Biopreparat was against the spirit of glasnost and perestroika, which had been proclaimed by Mikhail Gorbachev.

By 1988, the Institute of Ultra Pure Biological Preparations was working on refining the technology associated with biological weapons, while the Technological Bureau at Kirishi was working on developing new equipment to manufacture and deliver weapons. The Institute of Vaccines and Sera at Krasnoe Selo near Leningrad was essentially providing cover for the other plants by carrying out some civilian work on more conventional vaccines.

In May 1979, U.S. intelligence received the first reports of an explosion at a secret research facility known as Military Cantonment 19, or the Institute of Microbiology and Virology on the outskirts of Sverdlovsk, 850 miles east of Moscow. A leak of anthrax from the factory had killed up to a hundred people in the factory and in plants and houses downwind. The United States believed that up to 22 pounds of anthrax spores had been released into the air to contaminate an area three miles downwind of the factory. The Soviets had tried to contain the damage with a widespread immunization program that had proved largely ineffective.

Throughout the 1980s, the subject of the Sverdlovsk leak had been raised by British and American officials with their Soviet counterparts. Until 1992, the official line was that a handful of people had died in the city after eating contaminated meat bought on the black market. President Boris Yeltsin finally admitted the truth in June 1992, during an interview with *Komsomolskaya Pravda*, a Russian daily newspaper. The same newspaper had already printed an interview with General A. Mironyuk, a retired official from the Ural Military District, which controlled the Sverdlovsk area. He said he had learned from the KGB that "someone from the laboratory arrived early in the morning and began to work without turning on safety filters and other protective mechanisms. Only after they were pinned to the wall did the specialists confess. It was then that an entire program to disinform the public in the country and the world was developed."

Before that public admission, Western intelligence agencies had relied on snippets of information from sources in the Soviet Union and some satellite imagery that showed plants and testing sites apparently configured for the manufacture of biological weapons. The U.S. Defense Intelligence Agency produced a series of reports in the second half of the 1980s that estimated that the Soviets had up to eight sites for developing and storing biological weapons. The British SIS largely concurred with that view and a series of reports were circulated to the Joint Intelligence Committee and to senior officials in Washington and London, warning that the Soviet biological program had not slowed down as a result of the Gorbachev reforms.

As frequently happens when intelligence is fragmentary, the politicians refused to hear the message. At the time, all Western governments had been seduced by the reforms that Gorbachev was introducing across the Soviet Union. For the first time, there appeared to be a thaw in the Cold War, and no prime minister or president was prepared to risk a confrontation with the Soviets that might change the delicate balance of international relations. At the same time, there was a sense that Gorbachev was an honorable man who would not allow anything so terrible as biological weapons to be developed while he was president. As a result of these considerations, the intelligence warnings were ignored.

Then, in 1989, British intelligence was contacted by Vladimir Pasechnik, a senior official in the Biopreparat program who wanted to defect. He brought with him a complete picture of the program he had worked on for the past 15 years. He told a convincing tale of the most massive deception operation ever perpetrated by the Soviets and his evidence was so compelling that even the politicians who had no wish to confront Gorbachev were left with no choice. In April 1990, the British and U.S. governments presented a joint demarche to the Soviet Union which spelled out in detail what they knew. There was no reaction.

In June 1990, President Bush and Prime Minister Margaret Thatcher met separately with Mikhail Gorbachev and each raised the biological weapons issue. Although he must have been briefed by his own officials about the demarche, Gorbachev denied all knowledge of any such program. Thatcher, who believed she had an especially close relationship with the Russian premier, told him that unless the program was stopped, the West would go public. Gorbachev promised that he would look into the matter.

Two months later, Soviet foreign minister Eduard Shevardnadze sent a reply, rebutting the charges. By this time, the CIA and the SIS had added to their preliminary assessment and had produced an even more exhaustive briefing for Bush and Thatcher. Having succeeded in forcing action at the highest levels after so many years of frustration, the intelligence community was determined to press its case until the Soviets confessed.

In September 1991, a month after the attempted Moscow coup, the new British prime minister, John Major, met with Gorbachev in the Kremlin. Publicly, the two-hour meeting was confined to economic issues, but Major once again confronted him with the evidence of the secret weapons program. Again Gorbachev denied everything and reduced the normally unflappable Major to wave an angry finger in the face of the Russian leader. "We've got the goods on you," he shouted.

As the intelligence community continued adding to the file, the demarches to Moscow continued through the fall of Gorbachev and the rise to power of Boris Yeltsin. At the first summit since his accession to the presidency, Yeltsin met with Bush at Camp David for four hours on February 1, 1992. In advance of the meeting, U.S. diplomats in Moscow had made clear that the biological weapons program was a major stumbling block between the two allies and a gesture by Yeltsin in this area would be seen as a good sign of a new era in U.S.-Russian relations. This time Yeltsin came prepared and, for the first time, admitted that there had indeed been a secret program, and that he had ordered it to be shut down. He told Bush that he had asked for a detailed report of the program, which was submitted to Yeltsin in March 1992. Here, the military finally admitted that they had secretly developed bombs and missiles capable of carrying anthrax, tularemia and Q fever biological agents in defiance of international agreements.

To maintain the pressure, President Bush, in a report to Congress in March 1992, stated that the former Soviet Union had "an extensive ongoing offensive BW program," which violates the 1972 Biological and Toxin Weapons Convention. In April, Yeltsin signed a formal decree and the program was supposed to have been shut down.

But years of Soviet and Russian denials in the face of incontrovertible evidence had produced a strong sense of distrust in Washington and London. The British and U.S. governments determined to demand access to all the biological weapons development, production, and storage sites. Under the 1972 convention, the Russians were obliged to file a list of all sites with the United Nations. A first draft was drawn up in Moscow in the spring of 1992, which listed only 4 of the 20 known facilities that were a part of the Biopreparat program. In July, Sir Rodric Braithwaite, Britain's ambassador in Moscow, and James Collins, the deputy chief of mission at the U.S. embassy, met with senior Russian foreign ministry officials. They warned the Russians that if the list went to the UN, it would be publicly denounced by the British and U.S. governments.

Three reports were eventually prepared, each one failing to give a complete picture of the weapons program. In the end, the idea of submitting a detailed report to the UN appears to have been abandoned. Nonetheless, in September 1992, Russia agreed to allow full inspection of all its biological warfare facilities by both British and U.S. scientists. Because Russia had failed to admit the existence of many of the sites, the two Western nations found themselves arguing with the Russians about visiting rights to sites that the Russians did not acknowledge.

Since then, verification has proved almost impossible. Aside from the reported closing of the test site on Vozrozhdeniye Island in the Aral Sea, which is in the independent republic of Kazakhstan and outside Moscow's control, there has been no discernible change. To reinforce Western concerns, the CIA brought out a defector from the Biopreparat program in late 1992. Like Pasechnik, he was a very senior official in the organization who was able to confirm all details supplied by the earlier defector.

He also confirmed Western suspicions that, while Yeltsin was claiming the program had stopped, the research and development of new strains of genetically-engineered superweapons were continuing apace.

For the policymakers, this new set of revelations posed a difficult challenge. Initial approaches to Gorbachev had been kept secret, in case he was seen to be publicly bending to Western pressure. It was feared this could jeopardize his delicate relations with the military. The same concerns applied to Boris Yeltsin. Too much publicity about the program and Yeltsin's clear failure to tackle the problem might undermine his position as president of Russia.

It was decided to do nothing publicly on the assumption that Yeltsin was genuinely trying to shut the program down and in the hope that he might prevail. When Presidents Clinton and Yeltsin met in Vancouver in April 1993, biological warfare was on the agenda. Once again, Yeltsin assured an American president that all work had stopped. This time, Yeltsin was so convincing that even some of the most cynical in the intelligence community were inclined to believe him.[10]

Five months later, another defector from the Biopreparat project came to British intelligence. He was not of the same caliber as Pasechnik or the defector debriefed by the CIA. He added little to what was already known about the basic program, but he was able to tell his debriefers just what steps the Russian military had taken to keep the project going.

In every facility that had been opened for inspection to Western intelligence, the Russians had established convincing cover stories that made it appear as if each site had been converted to research or to the manufacture of vaccines. The secret work continued in parts of the sites that were never visited by the U.S. or British officials. At the same time, a new, secret facility was under construction at Lakhta near St. Petersburg. Far from the Biopreparat biological warfare program being shut down, it had in fact undergone considerable modernization and work was continuing as before, in defiance of Yeltsin's orders.

Since then, there have been a series of meetings between British and U.S. officials, which have usually been led on the U.S. side by Lynn Davis, the undersecretary of state for International Security Affairs. But at every stage of the talks, officials have been hamstrung by the lack of pressure points to employ against the Russians. The decision remains in force that publicity could have unfortunate side effects by exposing Yeltsin's own weakness as Russia's president. The Clinton administration is unwilling to employ sanctions, as that would produce the very publicity everyone is anxious to avoid, and the Russians clearly recognize that there is no serious downside to ignoring the entreaties of Davis and her colleagues.[11]

In the days of the Cold War, Soviet intransigence was simply a fact of life, although Moscow too was expected to follow certain standards on, for example, nonproliferation. But the post-Cold War world is very different. A cautious approach to the problem of proliferation has helped create exactly the kind of loosened constraints that everyone had hoped to avoid. The scale of the Biopreparat program was such that, without tight central controls, some leaks from the program to other countries were inevitable.

The threat of such leaks of material and expertise has been made more real by the parallel development of organized crime. For example, one organized crime company was established in Russia in 1992 with the aid of former KGB officials who had access to some of the secret funds the intelligence service had hidden overseas. Western intelligence expects that company to turn over some $4 billion in 1996—a budget much larger than that of the CIA. Business has flourished because the company has diversified its criminal activities, including money laundering, the supply of sophisticated armaments to China, North Korea, and Pakistan, and the development of extensive contacts with Iran.

# IRAN'S CW PROGRAM

It is this latter relationship that is of particular concern. According to senior Western intelligence officials, Iran has used the organized crime company to hire scientists knowledgeable about Russia's nuclear, chemical, and biological weapons programs and has also obtained raw materials from the same source.

In addition, German and Indian firms provided equipment and raw materials, normally used in pesticide plants, that have helped Iran develop CW. In May 1996, India concluded a $15 million deal with Iran to construct a plant at Qazvim, outside Tehran, to manufacture phosphorous pentasulfide. The chemical can be used to make pesticides, but has been identified by the Australia Group as a precursor for some chemical weapons.[12]

There are now four facilities in Iran capable of producing sarin, tabun, and mustard gas. The CIA also believes that Iran is working on binary nerve gas and is trying to acquire the capability to launch chemical and biological weapons with ballistic missiles. Iran's new chemical and biological weapons facilities are located in petrochemical plants in Bandar Abbas and at other sites. This not only makes the program difficult to track, but impossible for a country such as Israel to attack and destroy given the collateral damage they would inflict.[13]

Adding to concern in America and Europe is Iran's $40 billion arms buying program, which will transform it into the most power military force in the Middle East, with the possible exception of Israel. Apart from buying tanks, artillery, and fighters, Iran has purchased Scud B and C missiles from North Korea and is trying to develop its own ballistic missiles. Iran has also encouraged North Korea to develop a new generation of ballistic missiles, which will bring most of Europe within range.

As with Libya and Russia, administration officials are undecided about what action, if any, they can take against Iran to force it to stop its weapons programs. Sanctions are considered ineffective and counterproductive. Little diplomatic pressure can be applied to a country that is considered to be beyond the pale in the international community.

# THE PROLIFERATION CHALLENGE

The scale of the proliferation challenge was outlined by Secretary of Defense Perry in April 1996: "During the height of the Cold War, the Russian physicist Andre Sakharov said, 'Reducing the risk of annihilating humanity in a nuclear war carries an absolute priority over all other considerations.' The end of the Cold War has reduced the threat of global nuclear war, but today a new threat is rising from the global spread of nuclear, biological, and chemical weapons. Hostile groups and nations have tried or have been able to obtain these weapons, the technology, and the homegrown ability to make them or ballistic missiles that can deliver the massive annihilation, poison, and death of these weapons hundreds of miles away. For rogue nations, these weapons are a ticket to power, stature, and confidence in regional war."[14]

There is no doubt that the loosening of international constraints that marked the end of the Cold war poses series problems for the counterproliferation regime. The experiences in Russia, Libya, and Iran show clearly that current treaties, agreements, and punishments are inadequate to meet the threat. It is also clear that countries that operate outside the normal world of responsible governments pay little heed to the threat of sanctions (often because they are already in place). North Korea, for example, maintains an extensive CBW program and Syria is constructing a poison gas factory in Aleppo that is similar in scale to the one being built by the Libyans in Tarhuna.[15]

But it is important to keep this proliferation in perspective. As the Soviets discovered, having BW ambitions and realizing them with a weapon that can be suspended for delivery and then delivered effectively can involve a massive investment of time and money and the recruitment of top scientists. Acquiring an effective BW capability is not as simple as setting up a small laboratory in the basement and getting to work. On the contrary, it is a lengthy and complex problem.

# UNDERSTANDING CB TERRORISM

Equally terrible as the weapons may be, there is virtually no history of terrorists using unconventional weapons. In the thirty or so years since modern terrorism became a force, terrorists have tended to be conservative in their use of tactics and weapons. Today, terrorists still favor assassination, bombing, and the limited destruction of people and property over the use of weapons of mass destruction (WMD). It is remarkable, in fact, how little terrorism has evolved worldwide over nearly two generations.

But terrorism has also proved remarkably ineffective. The roll call of failed terrorist groups is a long one, the list of terrorists now in jail is also long, and the list of terrorists who have even partially succeeded in their aims is short. That suggests that terrorists will eventually change their tactics and move to a new generation of weapons. If that happens, it seems likely they will either attack in cyberspace or use weapons of mass destruction.

The experience in Japan notwithstanding, terrorist groups are more likely to acquire their WMD from friendly nations than they are to develop them alone, and it is here that the greatest danger lies. At present, the monitoring regime that checks on CBW proliferation is exceptionally porous and there is little disincentive for governments to hold on to the weapons they have. In fact, the lesson of the past few years is that there is no real price to be paid either for acquiring CBW or for passing them along to a friendly ally.

The Clinton administration has promised massive retaliation against any country using CBW, but this is a vague and barely articulated policy that bears no relation to the defined policy of Mutually Assured Destruction of the Cold War. Without some similar hard policy that exacts a heavy price from every proliferator, the further spread of CBW is inevitable. It is inevitable, too, that CBW will reach the hands of a terrorist or a rogue nation that will consider the use of CBW to be a legitimate act of war. By then, an effective counterproliferation regime will be too late.

# Notes

1.  "Generals Questioned Over Secret Chemical Weapons Project," South African Press Association, May 15, 1996.
2.  *Sunday Times* (London), February 26, 1995.
3.  Western intelligence sources, February, 1995.
4.  James Adams, *Engines of War*, (New York: Atlantic Monthly Press, 1990), pp. 240-246.
5.  James Adams, *The New Spies*, (London: Hutchinson, 1994), pp. 266-268; *Time*, April 1, 1996, pp. 46-47.
6.  Associated Press, April 23, 1996.
7.  *New York Times*, April 4, 1996.
8.  *Washington Times*, June 24, 1996.
9.  Adams, *The New Spies*, pp. 270-283.
10. *Sunday Times* (London), March 27, 1994.
11. Western intelligence sources, June, 1996.
12. *Washington Times*, June 23, 1996.
13. *Sunday Times* (London), February 5, 1995.
14. "Proliferation: Threat and Response", Office of the U.S. Secretary of Defense, April 1996, p. iii.
15. *Washington Times*, June 5, 1996.

# UNDERSTANDING THE LINK BETWEEN MOTIVES AND METHODS

BRIAN M. JENKINS

T he sudden emergence of chemical and biological (CB) terrorism as a prominent concern of public policy has fueled the perception that it is an entirely novel and also poorly understood problem. In fact, the analytical community has devoted much thought to assessing the possibility that terrorist groups, organized crime, or fanatical cults might acquire and use, or threaten to use, chemical, biological, radiological, or even improvised nuclear devices. According to a poll conducted in 1985 by *TVI Report*, a quarterly journal devoted to the study of political violence, 69 percent of the readers responding (mainly government officials and members of the research community) thought it likely that terrorists would employ chemical weapons by the end of the century, while the use of biological or nuclear weapons by the year 2000 was considered unlikely. Many, however, have refrained from extensive public discussion of CB terrorism out of a concern not to promote ideas in the mind of a perpetrator, or to inflame public fears.

It is also true that the analytical community has raised more questions than it has answered in attempting to understand the prospect of CB terrorism. There has been a largely theological debate among analysts of terrorism over the last two decades. On the one side are those who assert that because it hasn't happened it won't happen—the disbelievers. On the other side are those who ascribe to a more apocalyptic view and believe that if something bad can be done, inevitably someone bad will do it—Murphy's Law view. The Tokyo incident has now discredited the disbelievers in this debate. But it is by no means clear that it vindicates those who believe CB terrorism is inevitable.[1] What kind of a threshold has in fact been crossed? What kind of CB terrorism threat do we now face?

## Focusing on Motives

To answer these questions requires an understanding of many factors. Technical factors relate to the ease with which terrorists might acquire and use specific agents and weapons of chemical or biological warfare; policy factors include what governments might do to limit vulnerabilities; and political factors involve the motives guiding the behavior of terrorists. The focus here is on the political factors. The key question today is whether motives are changing—whether the constraints that have inhibited terrorist interest in massive destruction are eroding.

History provides some useful context. The 1995 Aum Shinrikyo attack on the Tokyo subway system is not the only data point for this analysis. A complete chronology of events over the last 25 years involving the criminal use of chemical or biological substances would include scores of events. Deranged individuals, criminal extortionists, and, in fewer cases, political extremists have plotted or threatened to use chemical or biological substances. In a much smaller number of incidents, plots and threats have turned to actual use, involving few fatalities.

What motives inspired these events? The most ambitious schemes were the products of madmen. A few were simple acts of murder aimed at specific individuals. The most frequent threats were made by criminal extortionists, who targeted public water supplies or, more frequently, food or beverages. Such malicious product tampering emerged in the 1980s as an increasingly common crime, whereby extortionists used or threatened to use readily available poisons, such as cyanide and strychnine, to contaminate commercial products. Although there have been hundreds of these acts, few of them were fatal. The motive behind these incidents was usually extortion; consumer goods were used as the vehicle for dissemination; food processing plants, beverage companies, and retail food chains were the targets; retail stores were the venue, and the general public was the potential victim.

In only a handful of incidents was the large-scale, indiscriminate use of CB agents either plotted or carried out. In 1978, members of the Jones Town cult engaged in murder-suicide using poisoned Kool-Aid. In 1985, the Rajneesh cult in Oregon plotted to poison food at restaurants with salmonella in order to make local townspeople ill on the day of a crucial referendum election that would decide the fate of the temple in the local neighborhood. A third incident was evidently connected with the 1993 bombing of the World Trade Center. In his sentencing statement, the presiding judge at the terrorists' trial indicated that the bomb had contained cyanide in sufficient quantity to contaminate the entire structure (the chemical agent was evidently and unexpectedly destroyed in the bomb blast itself). And the fourth incident was, of course, the 1995 attack on the Tokyo subway system.

Notably, all four of these incidents involved religious motivations. Three of them involved a fanatical cult whose members had isolated themselves from society. There is little evidence to suggest that other types of terrorists, including those who have used conventional weapons for decades, have taken anything other than a modest interest in CB agents. What accounts for this striking fact?

It is important to recognize that terrorists have always possessed the capacity to kill more people than they have actually killed. Only 20 percent of terrorist incidents have involved fatalities. Of those, most involved only one or two fatalities. If murder and mayhem were their primary objective, terrorists would certainly have killed many more people. The record of terrorism indicates that most of acts of terrorism involve only symbolic violence.

Moreover, exotic weaponry is hardly required for the purpose of killing large numbers of people. There is no substantial technical ceiling on the killing of large numbers of people with the traditional instruments of terror, which implies that technical constraints have not been the primary barrier to the use of massively destructive weapons by terrorists. We must look to self-imposed constraints.

Scrutiny of the memoirs of terrorists, their trial testimony, and their police interrogations is revealing on this score.[2] It uncovers a great many operations that were contemplated but not carried out largely because the violence was deemed counterproductive to the intended goal. Terrorists appear to treat violence as a volume control, not an on/off switch. They turn it up high enough to cause shock and alarm, but not so high as to induce widespread public revulsion and unleash a government crackdown. The record reveals a good deal of debate about what precisely is the right level of violence to frighten or coerce opponents, and what is the wrong level from the point of view of stimulating undesirable reactions.

Morality has also played an important role in the terrorist's calculation of what types and how much violence to apply—but morality of a particular type. Terrorists tend to see themselves as held to a higher moral standard than their targets. They often see themselves as champions of justice against a corrupt society or an iniquitous allocation of power or authority within a particular piece of territory. They do not typically conceive of themselves as savages or barbarians, free to wreak violence for the sake of violence. Rather, they tend to see themselves as warriors for a just cause, whose political objectives require that violence be used in discriminate and proportionate ways.

This warrior mentality is evident in the image many groups create for themselves. Banners like the "Irish Republican Army" and the "Red Brigades" are consciously chosen to invoke military units and purposes. They are used to establish group cohesion, shared goals, and the pretense of the legitimacy of military combatants.

Terrorists have also been careful not to alienate perceived constituents. They typically imagine that they have legions of supporters whom they represent as a kind of vanguard. Losing that constituency would compromise the movement. In their concern about the potentially damaging effects of publicity, terrorists often think like politicians: What does every single action accomplish in terms of constituency politics? Will it help our cause or hurt it? Will it reinforce or undermine my role as a leader of the movement? Could there be a damaging backlash?

## CB WEAPONS AND TERRORIST MOTIVATIONS

These constraints do not, of course, apply to all groups in equal measure. But their effect has been pronounced. To invoke the volume control analogy, massively destructive attacks are at too high a setting on the scale. They kill too many people and promise counterproductive results.

If the aim of the terrorist group is to promote public sympathy for a cause, it would not make sense for them to kill large numbers of the population where they are attempting to gain sympathy. Poisoning a city's water supply in the name of a popular front will not keep the front popular with the citizens of that city. If their aim is to promote group cohesion and minimize the risks that its least violent members might betray them, then the use of violence must be carefully calculated and calibrated; there must be consensus. If their aim is to establish legitimacy as a political actor, and reinforce their image as a moral force, then certain actions may be rejected as unacceptable. And if their aim is to survive and prevail, then action that provokes unprecedented government crackdowns must be avoided. Authorities in all political democracies operate under constraints. Any credible CB terrorist threat would change the rules quickly. Any barriers to the collection of domestic intelligence would evaporate. Some of the other factors that ordinarily constrain democratic societies in responding to terrorist threats would likely give way in the face of arguments about the societal stake in preventing or preempting actions that might kill thousands, indeed hundreds of thousands of people.

## ARE MOTIVES CHANGING?

How important are these constraints likely to be in the future? Will they operate as they have in the past to restrain the use of massively destructive weapons? Is the Aum Shinrikyo attack a sign of a new form of terrorism, or at least new terrorist actors and methods? If so, what are the implications for the future use of CB agents by terrorists?

The constraints, of course, are not immutable. In fact, there are suggestions that they are changing in worrisome ways. Revenge is a powerful motive, and becomes an increasingly important part of the calculus in the drawn-out conflicts between terrorist organizations and their opponents. A desperate group, persuaded that all is lost, may be driven by a desire to exact a terrible price for its defeat. Doomsday scenarios with doomsday finales become more likely.

The emergence of the far Right as a perpetrator of terrorism is also troublesome. Individuals and groups at that end of the political spectrum have a different concept of political power, in which they envision the emergence of leaders who will impose order on the despised masses. As a result, the Right has shown a greater willingness to undertake large-scale violence. Add to this mix notions of racial supremacy or ethnic hatreds that dehumanize victims, and the capacity for large-scale violence is magnified.

Moving into the realm of religious fanaticism, there are those who see God as the only constituent. Whether that god speaks through the mouth of some angry sheik, extremist rabbi, fundamentalist preacher, or mad guru in Tokyo, if he says that it is permissible to kill indiscriminately, then the constraints of conventional morality fall away.

Large-scale or indiscriminate attacks are, in fact, becoming more common, especially since the mid-1980s. The mode of attack has not been with chemical or biological weapons, but with car and truck bombs. With growing frequency, terrorists employ huge quantities of explosives on wheels for attacks on population centers or public symbols. In other cases, terrorists have exploded bombs in public places or sabotaged airplanes, all actions calculated to kill large numbers of people. This is a worldwide trend evident in both the recent suicide attacks in Israel and the 1995 summer bombing campaign in Paris.

This shift toward large-scale killing reflects a change from the ideologically-motivated terrorism of the 1970s and 1980s to a new set of motivations in the 1990s. Current conflicts are driven largely by racial or ethnic hatreds or by religious fanaticism. Atrocities have become almost commonplace. The historical record well documents the tendency of terrorists to mimic the behavior of others. Once a spectacular event has taken place, it is likely that a similar event will follow. The Aum's interest in chemical weapons seems, for example, to have been stimulated by the publicity surrounding the possible use of chemical weapons during the Persian Gulf war in 1991. We cannot know if at this very moment someone inspired by the Tokyo attack is busily planning to carry out something similar in the future.

## LOOKING TO THE FUTURE

It is essential to recognize the difference between a car bomb attack and a massively destructive chemical or biological attack. Both are indiscriminate, but the scale of potential casualties is very different. Even the Aum attack killed only a small number of people, however indiscriminate its method. This suggests that the principle lesson that many take from Aum—that it opens up a new era of massively destructive CB attack—is both unfounded and unwise. Constraints may be eroding, but they have not gone away. Contrary to what some assert, it is not just a matter of time before we witness an attempt at mass murder using chemical or biological weapons. Such an event may occur, but it cannot confidently be predicted on the basis of what we know today about the motives and interests of terrorists.

To be sure, history is full of many attempts at mass murder. But these are not indiscriminate acts, by and large. The practitioners of genocide have sought not the random removal of people but the elimination of particular people and groups. In the terrible examples we have in history of massacres and genocide in places like Rwanda, Cambodia, and Nazi Germany, the killing has been selective, even when the killing has been on an industrial scale. What are the signs of future terrorist acts of massive destruction and indiscriminate use of CB weapons for which we should be alert? What are the motivating factors that we must watch for in an individual or a group considering such an act of terrorism? One sign is the presence of notions of racial supremacy, ethnic hatred, or religious fanaticism. A second is deep-rooted hostility toward a specific ethnic group or government. A third is isolation—psychological, social, and geographic—as manifested in structures like compounds and mountain redoubts (although such isolation is just as possible in urban settings as in remote rural areas). A fourth sign is evidence of paranoid or conspiratorial thinking and the belief, often reinforced by group-think, that the group is under imminent attack. A fifth sign is apocalyptic or doomsday thinking. A sixth factor is the presence of a charismatic leader who demands and receives absolute obedience.

What are the future terrorist methods for which we should be prepared? How serious is the prospect of CB terrorism? The foregoing discussion of motives provides part of the answer: acts of CB terrorism may be growing more likely, but they remain at the edge of probability, especially those intended to cause large numbers of deaths. Moreover, technical factors remain an important constraint. It may be easy to acquire or fabricate chemical weapons or obtain dangerous biological agents in small quantities, but manufacturing, storing, and disseminating such agents in large quantities is difficult and dangerous. The lurid image created by media reports of the lunatic genius in his garage creating weapons that will kill millions is simply wrong. It is important in this regard to recall the details of the Tokyo chemical attack. It was perpetrated not by a solitary individual but by a well-financed, large, and scientifically-staffed organization. Even with its sophistication and resources, the group's attack was primitive and the casualties it caused were few. The attack's failure must be measured not least in the crackdown it generated and the termination of the cult's existence.

This line of argument points to a number of other predictions, however risky they may be. First, the future CB terrorist is more likely to threaten to use CB agents than to actually use them. The Aum attack supports this prediction by establishing a certain credibility to the threat; whereas in the past such threats might have been dismissed as crazy, they now must be taken seriously. Second, the use of chemicals will prove more prevalent than the use of biological substances. The Aum sect had the scientific, technical, and fiscal resources to produce biological agents, but they chose a chemical substance instead. Third, small-scale attacks are more likely than large-scale attacks. Fourth, chemicals that can be bought in an industrialized society, such as cyanide, strychnine, even rat poison are more likely to be used than more exotic weapons such as nerve agents or designer bugs. Fifth, crude dispersal in enclosed areas is the most likely form of attack, with casualties ranging anywhere from none to several thousand. Finally, while there may be other incidents involving chemical and biological substances in the near future, these are not going to become commonplace. CB terrorism is not about to become the car bomb of the 1990s.

## NOTES

1.  For my early contribution to this debate, see Brian M. Jenkins, "Will Terrorists Go Nuclear?" California Seminar on Arms Control and Foreign Policy, discussion paper no. 64, Santa Monica, October 1975.
2.  Brian M. Jenkins, "The Limits of Terror," *Harvard International Review*, vol. 17, no. 4 (Summer 1995).

# Analyzing Technical Constraints on Bio-Terrorism: Are They Still Important?

## Karl Lowe

The purpose of this paper is to inject balance into contemporary thinking about the ability of terrorists to carry out attacks with biological pathogens. An act of bio-terrorism is certainly possible and is indeed worrisome, but is laden with risks for those who would try it and is far from the simple "cookbook" effort commonly assumed. Consequently, the likelihood of such an attack may not be as great as generally perceived.

Before discussing bio-terrorism further, it is necessary to narrow its scope. In its broadest interpretation, bio-terrorism could encompass attacks on crops; sabotage of fuels and machinery; poisoning of food, water, and medicine; assassination attacks on individuals; and attacks on groups of people in conveyances, rooms, buildings, government or industrial complexes, or even whole cities. In this paper, biological attacks on targets other than humans and assassination attacks against single individuals are not included to keep the paper short enough to be useful.

Before assessing the prospect of bio-terrorism, it seems appropriate to address some common misconceptions. Conventional wisdom suggests that biological agents capable of killing or disabling tens of thousands of people can be created in one's own bathroom or kitchen, deposited in the water supply of a major city, and in a few hours the world will gasp in horror as the casualty list grows. Reality suggests otherwise, although biological pathogens can indeed be grown in one's own home. Some, like staphylococcus and streptococcus, grow there naturally and still others like *E. coli,* botulinum, SEB, and salmonella grow naturally in improperly handled or stored foods. Even anthrax can be cultured at home and castor beans, from which the principal ingredient of ricin is extracted, could be grown in gardens. Biological agents can be cultured, refined, and converted to weapons at home if one has the knowledge, criminal motivation, and access to necessary equipment. That combination significantly narrows the probability, although not the possibility, of bio-terrorism.

Let's first consider risks to a modern city's water supply. Although some harmful organisms, like cryptosporidium, grow naturally in water, most biological pathogens cannot survive in water, narrowing the choices available to a terrorist. All water borne organisms die in the presence of sunlight and chlorine, a characteristic that fortunately reduces the number of harmful organisms reaching modern homes and restaurants. The harm that can be done by organisms surviving the journey is dependent on dosage consumed, rate of consumption, and the recipient's resistance, factors that further reduce a water borne pathogen's viability as a weapon. Given the low survival rate of water borne pathogens in nature, the volume of agent a person or group would have to produce and deliver to inflict serious casualties exceeds what would be manageable by a single individual and would even be difficult for a group of the size that bombed the New York World Trade Center. Thus, infecting a city water supply is not as simple as commonly believed.

Even cholera, the deadliest of water borne agents, dies rapidly in clear water because it is highly sensitive to the ultraviolet radiation in sunlight. In murky, untreated water consumed by people with an unbalanced or inadequate diet, cholera is in its element, killing up to 60 percent of those infected and untreated. In chlorinated water, cholera dies much faster and even if it survives the tortuous journey from a reservoir to a person's stomach, cholera is dependent on stomach alkalinity to do real harm. Prompt rehydration of victims radically reduces the risk of death. This combination of impediments makes it unlikely that cholera would be effective against the population of a modern city. Terrorists might see advantages in delivering biological pathogens in aerosol form, rather than placing them in food, medicine, or water. Aerosols can cover larger areas and inflict more casualties. Aerosols can be delivered in either wet mist or dry powdery form. In dry form, they will generally be easier to transport and will travel farther on the wind, giving them the potential to inflict casualties over wider areas. To be delivered in dry form, pathogens require milling and drying, an increase in process complexity not readily managed with just "terrorist cookbook" knowledge.

Some believe that anyone who can grow a biological agent can also deliver it as an aerosol. Among the most fearful scenarios is a stealthy terrorist spraying a small vial or spray can of biological agent into a building's air handling system. Although an aerosolized pathogen can be sprayed into the air handling system of a building or conveyance, whether or not many casualties will result depends on a wide range of variables. As with water borne pathogens, an aerosolized agent's ability to do serious harm is a function of achieving the proper relationship of dosage to area attacked, the period over which a potentially harmful dose is inhaled, and each individual's natural or acquired protection and personal immunity level. Unless a terrorist has detailed technical information on the rate at which air is exchanged in a building or conveyance being attacked, the number of cubic feet of space serviced by the air handling system, and the dosage required to inflict a human casualty with the agent being used, the success of an attack depends on blind luck.

Delivery of an aerosol in the open is also possible, but requires an understanding of the effects of atmospheric conditions on the pathogen being used. If the wind is blowing away from the intended target or shifts during delivery, the sought-after effect might not be achieved. Not all people in the path of a biological agent cloud get the same dosage because the wind carries particles in uneven volumes. If a pathogen is delivered as a liquid spray, rather than in dry form, the aerosol cloud will not travel as far and the agent's efficiency in reaching the target population's lungs diminishes significantly with most agents. Most biological agents that perform better in wet form tend to have very long and hard-to-predict incubation spans and low expected mortality, making them less likely candidates for terrorism.

A third misconception is that the more toxic the agent, the more likely it is to inflict a casualty, regardless of its route of entry to the body. Some who hear statements like "botulinum toxin is the most toxic substance known to man" assume that makes botulinum ideal for terrorism. Fortunately, the volumes of botulinum toxin required to inflict a human casualty via the pulmonary route are so high that it would be difficult for a terrorist to transport and disseminate sufficient quantities to successfully attack a major public building or, even more difficult, people in open air. Ingested in food, the dosage of botulinum required to kill is significantly smaller and the speed of action is accelerated, but why go through all the trouble to grow *Clostridium botulinum* and extract toxin from its liquid slurry when there are readily available, very fast acting poisons on the open market? A terrorist's perception of the answer to that question is the likely determinant of whether using a biological agent is worth the extra trouble and risk.

A final misconception is that if a biological pathogen can be delivered as an aerosol, it is also contagious from person to person via the pulmonary route. Relatively few pathogens that have successfully been transformed into weapons are contagious and even fewer are spread via coughing or sneezing. Notable exceptions are plague and smallpox and perhaps glanders, whose transformation into aerosol weapons is sufficiently difficult that most countries have been unable to do it. Diseases commonly associated with foreign biological warfare programs such as anthrax, gas gangrene, tularemia, brucellosis, Q fever, and Venezuelan equine encephalomyelitis (VEE) are not transferable from person to person through the air.

To further organize our thinking on how likely bio-terrorism may be, we should focus in turn on capabilities of a potential terrorist, nature and size of the intended target, performance characteristics of the chosen agent, efficiency of the delivery means selected, and obstacles in the path of successful delivery. Likely terrorists fall into three broad categories, each with a very different capacity for inflicting harm. They include: (1) commandos, government agents, or sympathizers operating with a hostile state's sponsorship and assistance; (2) members of indigenous groups championing a cause or seeking to make a political statement; and (3) unaffiliated individuals with a score to settle or a burning desire to make a statement of their own. The greater the terrorists' access to or support by laboratories, the more comprehensive their knowledge of biological agent delivery requirements, and the greater their knowledge of infiltration and evasion techniques, the greater their chances of success. Fortunately, the combination of accesses, knowledge, and capabilities necessary for a successful terrorist attack is possessed by only a small number of people, few, if any, of whom are likely to be motivated to become a terrorist. The absence of successful bio-terror incidents to date is suggestive of how laden with unexpected twists the task may be.

If bio-terrorism were to occur, state-sponsored terrorists could be expected to do the greatest harm because they would presumably have the full support of the nation that sends them on their mission. Most likely, that includes producing a biological agent in the sponsoring country's biological warfare laboratories. Those facilities can be assumed capable of producing refined dry agent, deliverable in milled particles of the proper size for aerosol dissemination. Dry agent affords a terrorist several advantages. It is more easily transported and handled and requires a smaller volume to inflict casualties over larger areas. Ambitious regimes with frustrated agendas such as those in Iran, Iraq, Libya, North Korea, and Syria all have known or reasonably suspected biological warfare programs, ranging from applied research to production and storage. Although other countries are also known to have such programs, none seems likely to sponsor terrorism.

State-sponsored terrorists also have the advantage of access to training and technical advice from the sponsoring state, which overcomes guesswork on important technical details left out of commonly available "terrorist's cookbooks." Terrorist training would likely include delivery techniques, and skills such as stealthy entry and exit, self-protection, and target reconnaissance and surveillance. State sponsorship might also provide diplomatic cover, funding, clandestine transport of materials, and possibly escape assistance. All of that could heighten the likelihood of success.

There are, of course, risks that might make a state-sponsored biological attack less appealing. Most regimes likely to sponsor clandestine acts of violence against another country are themselves fearful for their survival. To remain in power, such regimes play off individuals against each other in their own government and sometimes within their own family, creating intense suspicion, internecine rivalries, and unforgiving grudges. Such leaders seem unlikely to trust *anyone* to get beyond reach carrying the means to destroy them and perhaps their entire government. Of course, the deliverer's family can be held hostage until the mission is carried out, the biological agent can be taken into the target country by diplomatic pouch, a religious or ethnic zealot bent on self-destruction could be induced to make the attack in order to eliminate the evidence trail, and the terrorist can be watched by "handlers," but there are still risks. Among the greatest risks is discovery. State-sponsored bio-terrorism might be viewed as an act of war that risks retaliation of the most serious kind. Because governments often behave unpredictably, sometimes reacting explosively to heinous acts committed against their people, no one can predict what might result. In the despot's calculus of possible costs versus benefits, even the most barbarous act of terrorism seems unlikely to produce a benefit worth risking a nuclear response. An act of bio-terrorism is recognized by many as having a "Pandora's box" effect unless punished by retaliation so severe that no one would ever risk trying it again. In this case, the punishment that best fits the crime is certainly not conventional.

A possibly less capable category of terrorists is an indigenous group with no ties to any government. Religious, political, anarchist, and even environmental groups generate an abundance of committed radicals intent on "bringing down the power structure." Such groups could have collective expertise in bio-agent production, targeting, and attack planning, although the expertise may not be sufficient to overcome problems posed in our earlier discussion of popular myths. A group of terrorists could also provide each other mutual support to acquire materials, reconnoiter the target, deliver the attack, and escape. They are most likely to produce a wet agent since drying a pathogen is likely to be lethal to the producer if not done in a carefully controlled environment by experienced people.

A glance into the Aum Shinrikyo cult's bio-production facility in Japan would reveal some startling violations of safety measures considered essential in U.S. laboratories. It should therefore come as no surprise that the cult's microbiologist died mysteriously and that the cult ultimately chose chemicals over biological agents to make their attack. No doubt someone with criminal interest is studying the Aum Shinrikyo case closely to avoid making the same mistakes, but given that pathogens, invisible to the unaided eye, are sufficiently intimidating to most people, terrorists are likely to be more confident of their ability to acquire, produce, and handle toxic chemicals.

Knowledgeable people argue that terrorists could reduce the risk of self-destruction by producing their own vaccines and testing them on small animals to determine dose requirements. While possible, that is not an undertaking for amateurs and the number of people with the requisite knowledge is fairly small, the overwhelming majority of whom are unlikely to ever become terrorists. There could, however, be a frustrated person who failed to get a sought-after research grant or promotion or was perhaps fired from a cherished job for reasons unrelated to professional expertise. It is also possible that such an individual could come into league with a hate group that needs his or her knowledge. Even if circumstances combined to put a revenge-bent maverick in a position to do harm, the person would also need criminal skills to avoid exposing the plot, narrowing the field still further.

Even if a usable vaccine is produced, there is still another concern for the terrorist producer of biological agents. Even the best vaccines can be overpowered by large doses of agent, a problem that makes most laboratories so concerned with safety. Because a biological agent's producers and deliverers are likely to come into contact with very high doses, they would be at extraordinary risk unless wearing a properly fitted mask whenever they are exposed (making it hard to remain unobtrusive when attempting to disseminate the agent). This is particularly true if the terrorist group wants to produce a dry agent since an electrostatic charge is imparted to particles during drying and humans attract them quite readily.

To avoid the time, cost, and risk associated with vaccine development, terrorists could take prophylactic doses of antibiotics to counter the effects of the pathogen they are developing or delivering. Medical texts contain information on types of antibiotics and dosage suited to particular diseases. As with vaccines, however, the exposure of developers and deliverers of pathogens could be considerably higher than the population they are trying to terrorize, requiring masks to help assure a textbook antibiotic regimen's chances of success. With some pathogens, antibiotics will not kill the organism, but will only block its reproduction, stopping the release of associated toxins while the antibiotic regimen continues. Strong antibiotics cannot be used indefinitely without causing serious side effects. When their use is discontinued, the pathogenic organism may resume reproducing, releasing toxins that kill. Again terrorists must arm themselves with very precise knowledge and adhere to high standards of safety if they hope to survive their own plot.

Since zealots sometimes don't care if they die, one could perhaps be persuaded to carry out a sacrificial attack. If the person producing and refining the agent is also the person who disseminates it, the risk of premature self-destruction is quite high. Fortunately, no one has yet succeeded in going very far beyond the laboratory research phase and those known to have done so delivered their attack without effect. A recent example was a group that intended to smear ricin on the doorknob of an official they disliked. With very few and exceedingly difficult to produce exceptions, biological agents do not enter the human body through unabraded skin. Unless the targeted person put his hand in his mouth after touching the doorknob, he would be unlikely to ingest ricin. Even touching a fork or spoon with contaminated hands might not do the job unless ricin was deposited on the portion of the utensil entering the mouth. Thus, the endeavor was dependent on blind luck, which fortunately smiled on the intended victim. Nor is it likely that a toxin deposited on a surface would aerosolize itself in the breeze and kill by entry through the lungs. Even if disseminated as an aerosol, the tendency for ricin to aggregate in particles too large to enter the lungs must be overcome, a technical challenge that still confounds countries with long-standing biological warfare programs.

The category of terrorist least likely to succeed in an act of bioterrorism is the unaffiliated individual. Such a person must know much about production, processing, dissemination characteristics, self-protection, and delivery techniques. With no assistance, an individual terrorist is left to do all the necessary targeting calculations, perform essential reconnaissance and surveillance of the target, and must successfully penetrate the area in which the attack is to take place and remain undiscovered long enough to carry out the act. The terrorist must also buy, steal, or make the agent, the delivery means, and necessary self-protection, all without unintentionally tipping off a curious person. In contrast to a group in which such tasks are distributed, the individual terrorist has formidable hurdles to overcome, making a bioterror attack by a lone individual the least likely to succeed.

After categorizing terrorists by their relative potential for doing harm, the next set of categories to consider is types of potential targets. These can be divided into three general categories: cities or other large open areas, buildings, and rooms. Attacking whole cities or other large open areas such as government or industrial complexes or airfields is a worrisome possibility, but would be difficult, although not impossible, for groups other than state-sponsored terrorists. Delivering dry anthrax from a truck, boat, or airplane is a nightmare scenario that cannot easily be prevented, but such an attack also has its problems, not least of which is the reality that those making the delivery require reliable protection for themselves unless they are intent on suicide. The second obstacle is putting the right amount of agent into the wind, high enough to cover the target, but not so high that it stays above the mixing layer of air to drift beyond the intended target. That requires the deliverer to have a good understanding of required dosage to inflict a casualty and the downwind performance characteristics of the agent, as well as fairly precise understanding of meteorology in play at the time of the intended attack. The description just offered fits a person who has a background in epidemiology and testing of aerosols for crop protection or biological warfare. The number of people with that combination of skills is very small indeed, making it likely that a terrorist would have to rely largely on luck to get it right. Releasing a vial of anthrax from the top of the Empire State Building is the popular image, but such an attack is very unlikely to succeed, even if it were possible during hours of darkness when the agent is most survivable.

Attacking a transportation terminal, office building, or industrial plant would encounter obstacles mentioned earlier. It is a technical problem to be worked out by seasoned people with a unique blend of experiences and expertise and must be carried out by a totally different kind of person possessing the physical agility, audacity, and savvy to reconnoiter and infiltrate the target area, deliver the agent undetected, and escape unnoticed. The harmonious blending of those personalities and capabilities is improbable, but not impossible. The same kinds of problems would exist if the target were a meeting room or similar target within a larger complex. The primary difference is the greater ease of concealing and disseminating the lesser volume of agent needed to successfully attack a smaller target.

Categorizing possible agents useful for a bio-terror attack could follow two courses. A common approach is scientific classification (bacteria, rickettsia, virus, toxin, ionophore, bioregulator, etc.), but that tells little about how useful an agent might be for a particular type of target. A more meaningful approach is to categorize agents by their operational performance characteristics, grouping them in terms of whether they are lethal or incapacitating, contagious or non-contagious, contagious via the pulmonary route or only through direct contact, and their expected performance as an aerosol in terms of the distance over which a specific amount can inflict harm on a desired percentage of those exposed. Instead of offering a menu of what to use against what type of target for best effect, it is sufficient to say that there are a relatively small number of biological agents that can be produced, refined, weaponized, and effectively disseminated by clandestine means unless a country with a biological warfare program is involved.

Now let's review some of the hurdles a terrorist might face in attempting to carry out a biological attack. The first obstacle is getting a starter culture of a pathogenic agent without arousing suspicion. Some have succeeded while others tipped their hand at the project's outset. The second obstacle is growing the agent in sufficient quantity to attack the intended target. That requires knowledge of lethal or incapacitating dosage, production efficiency, and the delivery efficiency of the chosen dissemination means. In the absence of that rare combination of knowledge, the terrorist could rely on luck and "cook up" a sufficiency for the target. A concurrent hurdle is staying alive while transforming the agent from a liquid slurry to a form suitable for dissemination. Although a common military mask is sufficient to keep aerosols out of the lungs, sheer volume of exposure in a makeshift laboratory poses a significant risk. The next hurdle is choosing a dissemination means suitable to the target and agent. Knowledge of necessary flow rates of aerosol dispensers relative to the volume per cubic meter of air to inflict casualties in the intended target area is a calculation few people understand. Even experienced scientists have differed in their interpretations of that calculus.

Even if all of the foregoing have been carried out flawlessly, the next set of hurdles cross from the technical/scientific realm to criminal skills, a combination rare in most people with bio-technical inclinations. The target must be thoroughly reconnoitered by the person or persons intending to carry out the attack, which must be done without arousing suspicion. Then, the terrorist must get into the proper location to deliver the attack without drawing attention. If it is intended to deliver the agent into the open air, precise knowledge of present meteorological conditions is necessary and self-protection is required if the terrorist wants to survive (some may not care). It is hard to imagine a person skulking about in a military mask without arousing suspicion. Taken together, the hurdles are formidable and the number of people who have the requisite combination of skills, knowledge, help, and motivation to carry out a successful act of biological terrorism is likely to be very small.

None of the foregoing suggests that bio-terrorism is impossible. It certainly is possible and the prospect is indeed worrisome, but there is a wide gap between possible and probable. Except for spurious acts of biological poisoning likely to affect small numbers of people, it seems unlikely that biological terrorism will achieve the fearful results popular misconception conjures. That is particularly true of lone terrorists or groups not linked to any government. Although the risks make state-sponsored bio-terrorism a questionable prospect, if countries with internationally banned biological warfare establishments ignore the risks and pursue bio-terrorism, the possibility of major casualties becomes much higher, a consideration suggesting serious review of civil defense and response measures in countries most likely to be targeted.

# BIBLIOGRAPHY

*Arms Control: U.S. and International Efforts to Ban Biological Weapons* (Washington, D.C.: GAO/NSIAD-93-113, December 1992).

*Chemical and Bacteriological (Biological) Weapons and the Effects of their Possible Use* (New York: United Nations Report #E.69.I.24).

*Countering the Chemical and Biological Weapons Threat in the Post-Soviet World* (Washington, D.C.: HASC Special Report #15, February 23, 1993).

Hoeprich, P. D. and Jordan, C. M., eds., *Infectious Diseases* (Philadelphia: J.B. Lippincott Co., 1989).

*Russian Foreign Intelligence Service Report on the Proliferation of Weapons of Mass Destruction* (Washington, D.C.: Senate Committee on Government Affairs, February 24, 1993).

Van Meter, C. T.; Krieger, K. A.; and Cleveland, P. R., *The Development and Use of Biological and Chemical Weapons* (Philadelphia: University of Pennsylvania, July 1964).

Westwood, John C. N., *The Hazard from Dangerous Exotic Diseases* (New York: Macmillan Press, 1980).

# Understanding Past Non-Use of CBW by Terrorists

## Ron Purver

Although terrorists have long demonstrated an interest in acquiring chemical and biological weapons and have sometimes used them, their resort to such use has been comparatively infrequent. Indeed, until recently, there has been a near total absence of the kind of mass-destruction attacks that some authors have long been predicting. However, most experts agree that the technical barriers to the acquisition and use of chemical or biological agents by terrorists are not particularly significant. If this is true—if the technical capacity to practice CB warfare is well within the reach of terrorist groups—then how does one explain the fact that the actual number of CB terrorist incidents has been relatively small when compared with the total number of terrorist incidents of all kinds; and that such incidents have almost all been limited to actions, if not threats, well below the threshold of "mass destruction"?

This chapter, drawn largely from a broader survey of the open (unclassified) literature on CB terrorism, will discuss each of the dozen or so explanations that have been given for why terrorist groups have not made greater use of chemical or biological agents in the past.[1] It will then briefly consider which of these perceived barriers or disincentives may be eroding, and which ones may still be operating to constrain the *future* use of CB agents by terrorists.

One explanation widely cited in the literature has to do with the fact that chemical and biological agents are uncontrollable once released into the environment. This seems especially apposite in the case of biological agents, often characterized as unpredictable due to their capacity to reproduce and their susceptibility to a wide variety of environmental conditions, such as wind, sunlight, and temperature. As described by some authors, the problem faced by the terrorist in contemplating the use of a biological agent is uncertainty about whether it will work at all, or whether its effects will be magnified well beyond the original intention. In the words of one study: "biological weapons...can produce negligible results, or a worldwide epidemic that makes no distinction between friend and foe."[2] The use of chemical agents, too, is judged by some authorities to involve many uncertainties flying in the face of an alleged terrorist tendency to "abhor uncertainty."[3] One author describes this latter characteristic as the desire for "premeditated control...over an event;"[4] another refers to the terrorists' general preference for "things that shed blood and go bang and explode in a fairly well-circumscribed time and place."[5]

The factor of unpredictability should not be exaggerated, of course. To some extent, it is shared by other types of weapons. Moreover, the perceived need for tight control over the results depends largely on the nature of the intended target—if the desired effect is to cause widespread destruction among an entire community, the ability to calibrate the effects of an attack may not be necessary. Indeed, some acts of terrorism may be designed precisely to maximize their indiscriminateness, whether to heighten public terror or cause the greatest damage.

Related to the unpredictability of the weapon is the oft-cited belief that terrorists fear for their own safety. To some extent, this fear may be well-founded; there have been numerous documented cases of accidental infections in the U.S. biological weapons program, for example. Nonetheless, some authors doubt that this is a concern of terrorists on the grounds that precautions, such as protective clothing, masks, or, in some cases, vaccines can be employed (albeit at some cost in terms of flexibility and mobility). Others point to the obvious fact that terror-ists who are willing to die for their cause (e.g., suicide bombers) are unlikely to be deterred by the risk of self-harm.

In seeking to explain the near absence of the use of CB weapons for purposes of mass destruction, many authors—especially those from the 1970s—referred to the simple fact that, historically, terrorist at-tacks had been specifically targeted and discriminate rather than indis-criminate in their effect. It was pointed out that, had it been otherwise, terrorists could have caused major disasters by attacking, for example, chemical plants or tankers with conventional weapons. Brian Jenkins has asserted that "simply killing a lot of people has seldom been one terrorist objective....Terrorists operate on the principle of the mini-mum force necessary."[6] Some authors speculated that, while a single individual might be willing to accept uncontrolled indiscriminate con-sequences, this was unlikely to be the case with an entire terrorist group. Disagreement about goals and methods would magnify problems of organizational cohesion and raise the possibility of defections. The danger of collateral damage to non-targets, including active supporters and potential sympathizers, was believed by some to be a disincentive to the terrorist use of infectious biological agents in particular.

Other authors have disagreed with this general characterization of terrorists as seeking to avoid widespread or indiscriminate killing. A number of recent spectacular incidents would appear to bear them out, including the World Trade Center bombing, intended to kill tens of thousands of individuals; the Aum Shinrikyo attack in Tokyo; and the Oklahoma City bombing. Clearly, not all terrorist groups are equally discriminate and there may, in fact, be a trend, for whatever reason, toward incidents of greater lethality and destructiveness.

Perhaps surprisingly, moral qualms are occasionally mentioned as a disincentive to terrorist use of CB agents. These presumably relate to the injury of innocent persons or the sheer scale and horrific nature of the damage or suffering inflicted. Biological agents might also be con-sidered iniquitous because they are likely to severely affect the elderly, the very young, and the infirm; as well as possibly pose a danger through secondary and tertiary outbreaks for years to come, perhaps even affecting future generations. Some authors have speculated that so-called "eco-terrorists" who would normally decry the desecration of the natural environment by chemical spills, etc., would naturally be loathe to employ CB agents that might harm the environment. It is unclear, however, whether this would affect their propensity to use chemical agents in "low-level" incidents directed at individuals or small numbers of people that would not have widespread environmental impact. In the case of BW, it has been suggested that radical animal rights activists might even fear the spread of a contagion from humans to other species.

Most authors quickly dismiss the notion that terrorists would be inhibited on moral grounds from the use of CB weapons. However, many authors believe that terrorists are inhibited from using CB weapons by the realization that any such use for mass destructive purposes would be counterproductive by alienating their followers or potential supporters, who would be morally revulsed by such use. These moral considerations are usually considered a constraint only insofar as they might threaten to erode the support of followers or potential members of a terrorist group that did employ such means. Of course, this assumes that the terrorist group in question is, in fact, sensitive to popular opinion, seeking to cultivate the support of, or at least to avoid antagonizing, those elements of the public that would consider the use of CBW to be morally abhorrent. Not all terrorist groups fall into this mold, however. Recently, we have witnessed the commission of acts designed solely to maximize terror or to achieve the greatest degree of disruption and/or destruction, regardless of the potentially negative impact on public opinion. At best, then, it can be said that many traditional terrorist groups seeking legitimacy from the world at large may be deterred by moral considerations from the use of CB agents. However, new and more frightening groups, with entirely different agendas, are emerging that may not be similarly swayed, even indirectly, by considerations of moral opprobrium.

Even the latter kind of terrorists, however, must presumably take into account the reaction of the targeted group or government to an attack of this nature. A surprising number of authors cite the anticipated severity of the governmental response to such an attack, perhaps even threatening the terrorist organization's very existence, as an additional factor inhibiting the terrorist use of CB weapons for mass destruction. In the words of one commentator: "Once political terrorists used mass-destruction weapons, the whole conception of the rules of the game would change."[7] On the other hand, others have made the valid point that it is often the purpose of a terrorist act to trigger excessively repressive countermeasures that, in turn, might so alienate the public as to help bring about the downfall of a target government, or at least drive a wedge between it and allied governments. The argument that terrorists are afraid of government response also fails to deal with those terrorist groups that may be acting out of sheer desperation or with no expectation of survival, as is the case with certain apocalyptic religious cults.

A recurring theme in much of the literature on the use of CBW is that terrorists so far have perceived no *need* to make use of such weapons in order to advance their goals. In the words of one author: "Terrorists have demonstrated repeatedly that their goals and objectives can be accomplished by using the same tactics and 'off-the-shelf' weapons...that they have traditionally relied upon....terrorists have yet to reach their killing potential using even 'off-the-shelf' weapons....the terrorists' traditional arsenal of the bomb and the gun still suffice to exact or win from governments the concessions that terrorists typically seek."[8] Against these statements, however, it can be argued that some terrorist groups, for whatever reason—whether the desire for greater notoriety because the public has grown inured to the traditional forms of terrorism and requires a more spectacular act to take notice, or because of a nihilistic view of life—may seek to distinguish themselves from typical terrorist acts of the past, and may consider CB agents the ideal means to do so.

Another aspect of the question of need relates to the type of *demands* that a terrorist group might make commensurate with the threat of mass destruction. Some authors discount the likelihood of such a threat on the grounds that there are few demands that would be both realistic in terms of what is being asked of the target government and credible in terms of a willingness to carry out the threat if their demands are denied. The single exception allowed by one author would be a demand for the release of political prisoners. Other analysts, however, have little difficulty in coming up with what they consider to be realistic demands by a group threatening CB terrorism, including, "a very large ransom, a demonstration of the government's impotence, and perhaps televised speeches of concession by government leaders."[9] The main problem with this line of argument, however, is that it fails to take into account groups that may not be interested in making specific demands of governments or whose only aim is to cause maximum destruction by striking without warning.

Yet another factor helping to explain the relative infrequency of the use of CB weapons by terrorists may be restraint on the part of state sponsors. While some authors credit the rise of state sponsorship with expanding the opportunities for CB terrorism through provision of the necessary materials and expertise, others are not so sure. It has been suggested, for example, that a state sponsor would wish at all costs to avoid being linked to and thus held even partially responsible for an act of such magnitude, given the likely severity of retaliation. A state sponsor might also be reluctant to relinquish control over such potent weapons out of fear that the terrorist group might engage in unauthorized use or even turn the weapons against the supplying state itself. A related factor mentioned by some authors is the difficulty a terrorist group might anticipate in finding a safe haven after committing such an act.

Prior to the Aum attack, another frequently-cited explanation was the simple lack of a precedent for an attack using chemical weapons. Conversely, many authorities anticipated the occurrence of copycat attacks following the successful use of CB agents. Some have gone further, pointing out that even an unsuccessful attempt might spark imitators by offering lessons to be learned for future attacks.

A final cluster of factors sometimes cited as inhibiting the terrorist use of CB weapons may be termed operational constraints. Although most authorities, as mentioned earlier, consider purely technical obstacles to the acquisition and use of CB agents by terrorists to be of relatively little significance, some do make the point that, in the words of one author, "the operation is far more complex than a shooting, kidnap, or hijack, and more likely to lead to failure or arrest."[10] A variation on this is the conviction expressed by another author that "Terrorists generally use the simplest technology available for their attacks....Simpler technology is less expensive and often more reliable. Low tech equipment is easier to obtain and attracts less attention....More important, the operatives who carry out the attacks need less training with low tech equipment."[11] Some authors attribute to terrorists a general reluctance to experiment with unfamiliar weapons.

Other, less prominent reasons given in the literature to explain the comparative lack of CB terrorist attacks in the past include:

1.  the fact that a terrorist group using BW agents might have difficulty in claiming credit for the outbreak of a naturally-occurring disease, although the inability to attribute the cause might also have its advantages for terrorists under certain circumstances;

2.  the contrast between a preference for sharp, dramatic impacts to exploit an event's immediate shock value, and the likely delayed impact and prolonged suffering anticipated as the result of most types of biological attack;

3.  the relatively large quantities of chemical agents that may be required to be effective; and

4.  the fact that the leader of such an attack would have to be suffering from a severe mental illness characterized by one author as "the very rare psychosis, organized paranoia," and the low likelihood that such an individual would combine charismatic appeal with technical sophistication and "the ability to sustain group commitment for an extended period focused on a difficult and risky task."[12] Interestingly, however, Shoko Asahara, the leader of the Aum Shinrikyo cult responsible for the world's first mass CB terrorist attack on a civilian population, appears to fit this profile almost perfectly.

To conclude, a search of the literature on the relatively low use of CBW to date yields explanations that can be placed into roughly four categories. First are those which, despite being mentioned in the literature, appear to carry little weight, attracting scant support from the majority of authors on the subject. Into this category might be placed the argument about the possible moral compunctions of terrorists.

The second category comprises factors that depend on the nature and goals of the terrorist group in question. For example, the fear of alienating public opinion would apply only in the case of a group seeking political legitimacy or dependent on a broader constituency for the achievement of its goals. Similarly, the alleged lack of suitable or commensurate demands, as well as the difficulty in making a threat credible, would be relevant only in cases where the terrorist group does in fact seek to have specific demands satisfied in return for not carrying out a threatened act. Restraint by state sponsors would obviously be operative only where a group is in fact state-sponsored or lacks the means of acquiring and using CB agents on its own. The related fear of difficulty in finding a safe haven or of inadvertent self-harm would not be a factor in the case of individuals or groups fully prepared to sacrifice themselves. Finally, the perceived lack of control over the possible effects of the use of such weapons would hardly deter a group intent on widespread and indiscriminate killing.

The third category contains explanations that appear to be losing their cogency in the face of recent trends, including such factors as the alleged traditional disinclination towards mass or indiscriminate killing; the absence of a need to resort to CB weaponry in order to advance their goals; the closely-related, alleged attributes of satisfaction with existing methods and the purported reluctance to experiment with unfamiliar weapons; the perceived lack of a precedent, particularly in light of the Aum Shinrikyo attack; and again considering the Aum Shinrikyo attack, the unlikely confluence of paranoid, charismatic leaders with access to the necessary technical expertise and other resources.

The fourth category includes factors that apparently continue to exert a constraining influence on terrorists generally, such as the difficulty of ensuring group cohesion in support of a possibly controversial policy; fear of government retribution; and the technical constraints that—although perhaps not insurmountable—nevertheless add to the complexity and risks of a planned operation, reducing its flexibility and increasing the chances of failure.

In short, it can be seen that numerous factors constraining the terrorist use of CB weapons may continue to apply, depending—and this is crucial—on the nature and goals of the terrorist group in question. However, a sufficient number of countervailing trends has resulted in the erosion of important past constraints, lending strong support to the widespread consensus among analysts that the likelihood of terrorist use of CB agents in the future is both real and growing.

## NOTES

1. Ron Purver, *Chemical and Biological Terrorism: The Threat According to the Open Literature*, Ottawa: Canadian Security Intelligence Service, June 1995.
2. Brian M. Jenkins and Alfred P. Rubin, "New Vulnerabilities and the Acquisition of New Weapons by Nongovernment Groups," in: *Legal Aspects of International Terrorism*, Alona E. Evans and John F. Murphy, eds., (Lexington, MA: Lexington Books), p. 225.
3. Brian M. Jenkins, quoted in: Patrick G. Marshall, "Obstacles to Bio-Chemical Disarmament," *Editorial Research Reports*, vol. 1, no. 24, (June 29, 1990), pp. 372-373.
4. Christopher C. Joyner, "Chemoterrorism: Rethinking the Reality of the Threat," in: *The 1988-1989 Annual on Terrorism*, Yonah Alexander and H. Foxman, eds., (The Netherlands: Kluwer Academic Publishers, 1990), p. 137.
5. Stanley L. Wiener, "Chemical and Biological Weapons and Terrorism", in: *International Terrorism: Policy Implications*, Susan Flood, ed., (Chicago: Office of International Criminal Justice, University of Illinois at Chicago, 1991), p. 70.
6. Quoted in: Bruce Hoffman, "Terrorist Targeting," in: *Terrorism and Political Violence*, vol. 5, no. 2, (Summer 1993), p. 23.
7. B. David, "The Capability and Motivation of Terrorist Organizations to Use Mass-Destruction Weapons," in: *On Terrorism and Combating Terrorism*, Ariel Merari, ed., (Frederick, MD: University Publications of America, 1985), pp. 150-151.
8. Brian Jenkins, quoted in: Hoffman, "Terrorist Targeting", pp. 22-23.
9. Elliott Hurwitz, "Terrorists and Chemical/Biological Weapons," *Naval War College Review*, vol. 35, no. 3 (May-June 1982), p. 37.
10. Richard Clutterbuck, *Terrorism in an Unstable World*, (London: Routledge, 1994), p. 53.
11. L. Paul Bremer, III, "Testimony...on High Technology Terrorism before the Subcommittee on Technology and the Law, Committee on the Judiciary, May 19, 1988," in: *Terrorism and Technology*, U.S. Department of Justice, Federal Bureau of Investigations, Office of the Executive Assistant Director Investigations, (May 19, 1988), pp. 2-3.
12. B. J. Berkowitz, et al., *Superviolence: The Civil Threat of Mass Destruction Weapons*, (Santa Barbara, CA; ADCON Corporation, Report A72-034-10, September 29, 1972), pp. IX-18; pp. 22-23.

# DEBATING POLICY PRIORITIES AND IMPLICATIONS

## ANTHONY FAINBERG

M ajor international terrorist activity arrived on U.S. soil in 1993, marked by the attacks on the World Trade Center in February and on employees entering the Central Intelligence Agency in March. These events demonstrated that the logistical and defensive barriers that apparently had earlier served to impede such attacks had been overcome.

On March 25, 1995, in an attack which holds important implications for U.S. national security, sarin, a chemical nerve agent, was dispersed in several trains of the Tokyo subway system. The terrorist conspiracy behind this act was the work of a bizarre, apocalyptic cult, called Aum Shinrikyo. This attack demonstrated that the strategic, tactical, and moral barriers that were thought to have dissuaded terrorist groups from using weapons of mass destruction had, at least in this case, been breached.

In the following month, April 1995, the bombing of the Alfred P. Murrah Federal Building in Oklahoma City became a stunning reminder of the presence of terrorism in this country. Many experts had initially suspected that this crime had its origins in the Middle East. However, the subsequent arrest and indictments of three American neo-fascists indicated that, unlike the bombing of the World Trade Center, this event was probably the result of a domestic conspiracy. Later in 1995, three other noteworthy cases occurred. In these, biological agents were illegally acquired by U.S. citizens, possibly for terrorist purposes. In two of these cases, the criminals were members of American neo-fascist groups and in the third, there was some circumstantial evidence indicating a connection between the arrested individual and right-wing survivalists.

These paragraphs outline the major U.S. terrorist events that took place in the past two years, following many years of decline in significant terrorism. The sources of these attacks were divided between international terrorists from the Middle East and U.S. right-wing extremists. Although terrorism from other sources cannot be excluded, ongoing activity from these sources is the principal threat facing the U.S. today.

A disturbing and recent development in terrorism has been the significant use of chemical agents for terrorist acts, although not in the United States. Furthermore, there is solid evidence of preparations for biological terrorism based in the United States.

This chapter addresses some of the policy implications of this turn of events. It begins with an attempt to frame CB terrorism in terms relevant to policy, so that specific parts of the problem can be addressed separately. It turns then to an assessment of the likely perpetrators of CB terrorism, arguing that the emerging problem is posed by those on the Right of the political spectrum, not the Left. The chapter closes with a discussion of policy priorities.

## HOW REAL IS THE THREAT?

In planning responses to terrorist attacks there is a danger analogous to that of generals who busy themselves planning to fight the last war. Future terrorist attacks may replicate history in their scope or tactics, but it is more likely that they will involve a broader diversity of measures and tactics. It is, therefore, complicated to plan for the next major change in terrorist techniques and tactics. We should consider, for example, the possibility of biological attacks against economic targets, such as crops or livestock.

History does present a guide to the kinds of threats that must be guarded against. However, governments cannot restrict their thinking to the past, but must anticipate future changes and trends in order to deal with them effectively. This will mean increased attention to the possibility that chemical or biological weapons may be used in terrorist attacks. In fact, governments are now, although somewhat ponderously, moving to take this threat into account.

Waves of terrorism in the 1960s and 1970s included some horrible novelties, such as blowing up civilian aircraft in flight (indeed, sometimes the aircraft even belonged to professionally neutral states, such as Switzerland and Austria). The decision by many groups to adopt this tactic (still pursued today) was a shock to the world community, which, three decades later, still has not adequately met this security challenge. The occasional practice of kidnapping and murdering major political figures or, in the case of the Munich Olympics, international athletes, has also shocked the world. This practice was not nearly as innovative as destroying aircraft—kidnapping and murder are, after all, part of a millennia-old tradition—but the world community was not prepared for such behavior and was rightly appalled. Since then, the security business has greatly expanded, if not been invented anew, in an attempt to deal with these kinds of attacks.

What more can terrorists do to attract attention? The standard tactics are bombings of various sorts, arson, kidnapping, and murder. If there is any recent trend, given the limited statistics on domestic terrorism in the United States, it may be the more frenetic attempts to draw the attention of the world media by acts that are ever more spectacular and cause massive numbers of deaths. It could be argued that for some terrorist groups any action resulting in less than the murder of scores of people is not effective, probably because not enough attention would be drawn to the perpetrators and their political goals. Into this category of spectacular events can be included the Lockerbie and UTA bombings, the attempt to destroy the World Trade Center, with the goal of causing thousands of deaths while destroying the twin icons of world capitalism, the bombing of the Alfred P. Murrah Federal Building in Oklahoma City, the wave of massive bus and other public bombings in Israel in 1996, and, I would argue, the attempt by a peculiar and irrational cult to kill thousands of innocent Japanese citizens.

Only the attack on Japanese citizens used a radically different weapon: the chemical nerve agent, sarin. We do not know whether this act presages imitative attacks by self-selected terrorist groups all over the world, using this or other weapons of mass destruction. *What has been proven, however, is that it IS possible for a subnational group (albeit a very rich and powerful one) to produce and use such weapons against the public*, even though the attack was bungled in many respects and was far less successful in causing deaths than it might have been. The chemical agents of possible interest are many and diverse, although the most likely agents to be used, based on ease of acquisition, include sarin, tabun, and other gases.[1] Likely biological agents include botulinum toxin, ricin, anthrax, plague, tularemia, and a number of other diseases.

We also can safely assume that this subnational terrorist "breakthrough" has not been lost on a large number of people who are in the terrorist business. Most of them will almost certainly continue to avoid the use of such weapons for a variety of reasons: the old-fashioned methods were suitable for the goals of most; there may be a reluctance to experiment with new and dangerous methods; the nature of the acts might alienate the terrorists from their base of support; the use of such weapons might bring down the wrath of governments and, indeed, most of the world upon the terrorists' heads.[2] All of these reasons are sound, and all make sense to most rational actors—and most terrorists need to be rational at some basic level, if only to survive.

Such reasoning is not universally applicable, however, as the Aum experience demonstrates. Some terrorist groups may not be directed by rational actors. For this reason, and because the precedent has now been set, responsible governments cannot ignore the possibility that terrorists may use chemical or biological agents to mount further attacks. While this may never happen (although the chances of attempts occurring within the next few years appear to be good), it does mean that responsible societies have to prepare themselves for this eventuality. What resources should be expended to this end is a matter for political discussion, one which this paper will attempt to probe. This is a typical risk assessment problem: how does one deal with events of low probability but high consequence? The policy response is clearly subjective, and whatever one suggests may be fairly subject to a critique.

## WHO CONSTITUTES THE THREAT?

A review of the major recent events which have involved the use or potential use of weapons of mass destruction indicates that such threats come from religious cults or neo-fascists, or from groups that are a combination of the two. This statement is based on few incidents and limited statistics and does not exclude the possibility that other groups may decide to use this terrorist option. In fact, there is some indication that Middle Eastern terrorists may be considering the use or threat of use of such agents.

An early case of potential use of biological weapons (in the 1970s) involved a small fascist group in Missouri called the Order of the Rising Sun, which was caught cultivating a large amount of typhus bacilli. A second early example (an exception to the "rule," since it involved an extreme left-wing, secular group) was the raid in 1982 on a Paris laboratory used by the Baader-Meinhof gang, which was found to have a significant amount of *clostridium botulinum*, the organism that produces botulinum toxin. In 1985, the Rajneesh religious cult in Oregon was accused by authorities of having poisoned hundreds of citizens by distributing salmonella at a salad bar, in order to influence the outcome of local elections by reducing the turnout of its adversaries. No fatalities or serious illnesses ensued, but many of people apparently stayed away from the polls and the Rajneesh did well in that election.[3]

A later example in March 1995 is the infamous Aum Shinrikyo attack, which used several types of chemical agents and may have, according to some unsubstantiated reports, attempted the use of anthrax or botulinum toxin as well. What are the characteristics of this particular organization? The Aum is a religious cult which combines a pot-pourri of religious and political beliefs, comprising, in the former instance, extracts from Hinduism and Buddhism, and in the latter, some extreme anti-American attitudes that extend to Nazi-like beliefs, particularly regarding Jews. Its leader makes some claims to divinity and the group was run in an extremely authoritarian, not to say thuggish, manner. Apparently, dissidents within and opponents outside the group were routinely targeted for murder and, in fact, many were killed.

In the United States, there is an interesting variant on the phenomenon of extreme religious and political groups. As noted above, the Rajneesh, a strange authoritarian cult of Hindu origin, which may have been chiefly commercial and capitalist rather than spiritual in orientation, did, in fact, use biological agents for political purposes, although perhaps not strictly as terrorism, per se. There are a number of other extreme rightist organizations in which there is demonstrated interest in the use of chemical or biological weapons. The case of Leroy Harris, associated with the Aryan Nation organization of Hayden Lake, Idaho, is one clear example—the Aryan Nation is a neo-Nazi group with a patina of fundamentalist Christian pretensions. Also noteworthy is the appearance of recipe books on how to make chemical or biological agents in extreme right-wing catalogs, which also sell other criminal handbooks, Nazi regalia, and the fascist tract-cum-novel, *The Turner Diaries*.[4]

These U.S. groups are unapologetically Nazi-oriented political and religious movements, in some respects resurrections of the Ku Klux Klan, which had been decimated by a series of wrongful death and wrongful injury lawsuits.[5] They include a strong component of fundamentalist religion in their *Weltanschauung*, but the religion is Christian, rather than Buddhist- or Hindu-based. They, like Aum, include extreme anti-Jewish and anti-United States (especially anti-democracy, as practiced in the United States) attitudes in their panoply of beliefs. This anti-U.S. point of view is sometimes disguised as being merely opposed to the current federal government, but, in reality, it has been manifestly anti-government on all levels. The fundamental adversary for them is not really the U.S. government, but the U.S. body politic and democratic system, to which these organizations are venomously hostile.

Some of these groups, including the Aryan Nation and various Christian Identity subgroups, are also characterized by individual leaders (Richard Butler in the former case, and Robert Millar in the Elohim City branch of Christian Identity) who operate in a starkly authoritarian manner, although nothing like the control exerted over the Aum by Shoko Asahara seems to exist.

There are a number of reasons for interest in these right-wing groups. Three events in 1995 involved acquisition of biological agents by individuals. All appear to have a tie to this end of the political spectrum. In the first case, several members of a so-called Patriot's Council in Minnesota were convicted of acquisition of ricin, a deadly biological toxin extracted from castor beans.[6] This poison has been used by at least one former Soviet-directed intelligence service (the Bulgarian, in the famous Markov murder) for targeting overseas opponents, but its use for mass killing may be technically problematic. The Patriot's Council was a small, extreme rightist anti-tax group, and the ricin was apparently meant for use against local officials of whom the organization did not approve.[7]

Later in the year, Leroy Harris, a member of the Aryan Nation, was arrested and charged with misrepresentation in acquiring freeze-dried *yersinia pestis* (plague) bacteria. A technician working in a small biological firm, he misappropriated a sheet of letterhead from his place of work to order the material from a Maryland laboratory, which supplies various cultures to researchers.[8] He was not charged with acquiring or possessing the bacteria, because at that time there was no law forbidding such possession unless there was also evidence of intent to use the material in a criminal act.[9] Harris asserted he needed the material to find means of countering a plague attack by Saddam Hussein on the United States, but this defense was hardly taken seriously, particularly since he had no real experience or knowledge in this area.[10]

The third case involved David Lawy, who was arrested in Arkansas in December with a large supply of ricin and castor beans. Lawy was thought to have ties to right-wing "survivalist" groups in the area, but nothing definitive was released to the public at the time. He claimed to be using the agent to poison coyotes (another rather implausible story) and committed suicide in prison within a few days. He was found to have in his possession several books marketed by the extreme right-wing press that describe how to manufacture poisons (including ricin), nerve agents, and the like.[11]

While three events do not confirm a pattern, they may indicate a trend: the interest of these groups in the use of weapons of mass destruction for terrorist purposes. Particularly of interest is the availability and use of "cookbooks," marketed by, for example, Paladin Press and Delta Press, that are able to give at least rudimentary advice on how to manufacture some chemical and biological agents and how to disperse them.[12]

Additionally, the threat from such groups is by no means restricted to weapons of mass destruction. Timothy McVeigh and Terry Nichols, indicted for the Oklahoma City bombing on April 19, 1995, had been in contact with extremist right-wing militias. McVeigh had been in touch with a Christian Identity sect located near the Oklahoma-Arkansas border just before the bombing.[13] He had for months pushed *The Turner Diaries* on his friends. Interestingly, the precipitating event for the Nazi insurrection described in that book was the bombing of a federal building (the FBI headquarters in Washington), an event that had many details in common with the Oklahoma City attack.

In summary, the *domestic terrorist threat* from a plethora of neo-fascist groups in the United States is real. Minor bombings of federal buildings around the country have continued in the months following Oklahoma City. Three sets of arrests appear to confirm the interest of some members of such groups in biological and chemical weapons, as do a number of "how-to" publications distributed by extremist presses.

There is also an international terrorist threat against the United States. Judging from recent events, principally the conspiracy of the gang around Shaykh Umar Abd-al Rahman to bomb the World Trade Center and other targets in New York, the mode of operation appears to be more classically terrorist: the use of bombs, rather than more exotic weapons. The one exception to this might be indicated by a letter written by Ramzi Ahmed Yussef (being tried for a major role in the World Trade Center bombing, and accused of having intended to blow up several U.S. aircraft in flight in the winter of 1994-95) threatening to use chemical weapons against the Philippines government if a friend was not released from prison. This letter may not even have been sent, however.[14] In the absence of further evidence, although there is a very real international terrorist threat against the United States, there is, as yet, little evidence that this threat includes the use of weapons of mass destruction.

## POLICY PRIORITIES

### 1. FIX THE INTELLIGENCE PROBLEM

Of the several levels of government response to any terrorist threat, the first is adequate intelligence. Understanding the motivations of terrorists is vital in order to understand whether, where, and when the chemical or biological option is a serious threat. For example, some recent suicide terrorism in Israel might, by extension, indicate that a terrorist group may resort to the use of chemical or biological agents in spite of serious danger to its own agents. If so, one of the main obstacles to the use of such weapons by terrorist groups may be overcome.

It was disturbing that the U.S. intelligence community did not have any serious information about Aum Shinrikyo in March 1995, even though their possible role in the release of sarin in Matsumoto, Japan, during the previous summer had been widely discussed in Japan. Defenders of the intelligence community note that it is, of course, impossible to monitor every bizarre religious group. While this is true, it should be possible to monitor every bizarre religious group that is thought to have had a role in releasing sarin to the general public.

The incompetent behavior of Japanese law enforcement authorities (far more serious that the lapses of overseas intelligence communities) regarding the Aum, after the Matsumoto release, still has not been fully understood. However, it is likely that one reason for their reluctance to pursue the group more actively was that it was a religious group, and matters of religious freedom are taken very seriously in Japan. The same is true in the United States, where federal authorities must have some evidence of conspiracy to commit illegal acts in order for law enforcement agencies to take serious intelligence measures. While difficult to prove, it seems likely that if an organization is religious in nature, or at least claims a quasi-religious basis for its philosophy, many law enforcement decision makers will require stronger evidence of illegal intent before beginning to gather intelligence on their activities.

There should be a conscious decision to treat religious organizations on the same basis as any other organization when it comes to illegal activities, particularly conspiracies to commit violence. This may imply an active program to gather information on a number of groups that have been involved in violence of a political nature or whose rhetoric plausibly indicates an intent to commit further violence.

In fact, it should become normal practice to monitor the activities of large, well-heeled extremist groups overseas, whether or not they are religious in nature. As a practical matter, even with the expertise and resources upon which the Aum could call, their attack was not nearly as successful as it might have been: thousands, rather than twelve, could have died under a better executed plan. Efforts by small, less prominent groups will likely experience at least the same level of difficulty that the Aum did, due to organizational problems and to impulsive decisions by a small, and quite possibly, unstable leadership. This does not mean that it is impossible for a much smaller group than Aum to mount a successful chemical or biological attack. But the likelihood of a major success is much greater, given a large organization with significant resources and expertise.

In the Aum case (admittedly in retrospect), the group exhibited many indicators that should have attracted interest. For example, they had over a billion dollars in assets, claim tens of thousands of members (more of whom were Russian than Japanese), and broadcast strange propaganda from a radio station in Vladivostok and a television station in Moscow. After suspicions in Japan were raised by the Matsumoto incident (and remarked upon by a U.S. researcher, Kyle Olson, who actually warned of a potential Aum attack on the Tokyo subway system), it is difficult to understand why U.S. intelligence officials were not following the matter more closely. Clearly the intelligence community will be more sensitive to this problem now and will be more active in seeking out information in such cases. I hope and imagine that this decision has already been taken.

But the intelligence problem is not fixed simply by gathering information on a wider group of organizations. Sound analysis is also required. This requires interagency coordination. In the latter field, it is especially vital to coordinate the overseas intelligence capabilities of the government with the intelligence units of domestic law enforcement agencies, especially since there has recently been a strong international component to domestic terrorism in the United States.

Ongoing intergovernmental exchanges of information are vital to this process. There is an urgent priority to promote more effective collaboration. In some specific cases, there are useful exchanges of information and technology that take place on a bilateral basis between the United States and another country. In others, there are multilateral arrangements to this end. Real advantages may accrue from proper sharing of information on terrorist groups, their motivations and activities, as well as sharing information on counterterrorism training techniques. Since enhancing response capability has been identified as a major requirement, an advantage of international discussions would be the incorporation of different views on the training of responders.

## 2. Address the Needs of First Responders

There is a clear need to improve the ability of first responders. Many observers have been struck by a media image from Tokyo, in which a protected medical technician, responding to the sarin attack, was accompanied by an unprotected policeman. The potentially disastrous consequences of such procedures are clear. There is widespread concern that local emergency personnel in the United States are currently similarly unequipped and unprepared to respond properly to chemical or biological terrorism. Local forces need protective equipment, basic chemical and biological agent detectors, and, above all, training. At a recent exercise in New York City in which an attack was postulated in the subway system, most first responders were nearly immediately declared "dead." The response team in this case was considered to be one of the better prepared forces for such an eventuality. In many areas, it is not even clear how long it would take local firefighters or law enforcement authorities to recognize (by victims' symptoms or other means) that chemical or biological agents were responsible for mass casualties. This serious gap in incident response is in need of urgent remediation.

The Office of Emergency Preparedness (OEP) of the Department of Health and Human Services has already designed a plan aimed at improving the capabilities of first responders. It emphasizes specially-trained and well-equipped metropolitan strike teams. The plan envisions such teams in 17 major urban regions. This plan leaves largely unaddressed the problem of attacks in urban areas not among the 17 and in regions not adjacent to the selected urban centers. Perhaps the metropolitan teams should, therefore, have some regional responsibilities as well.

The OEP plan has suffered huge difficulties in moving from conception to implementation. Most of the difficulties have to do with money. At one point in the 1995-96 congressional budget battles, this office was actually zeroed out of existence. Only after extended arguments on Capitol Hill were $5 million of the requested $9 million restored. When one considers this congressional behavior against the backdrop of the world's first major terrorist attack using weapons of mass destruction occurring only a few months earlier, one is impelled to conclude that there is an appalling ignorance on the part of some congressional staff. This ignorance may simply be due to understaffing and overwork, it may be due to incompetence among key staffers, or it may be ideological in nature, wherein the unique guiding principle for all action may be to downsize government. But whatever the reason, the resulting action in this particular case has been manifestly pernicious and damaging to the national security. Clearly, if there is a threat of biological terrorism (and we have seen that the threat does exist, although the degree of likelihood may be a matter of discussion), the correct response is hardly to render the nation vulnerable in order to save a small amount of money.

## 3. REMOVE THE BARRIERS TO A COORDINATED GOVERNMENT RESPONSE

Policymakers must also look beyond the task of treating first casualties to the larger challenges of consequence management. These are only in part public health tasks and they raise bureaucratically sensitive issues about who controls what.

Independent observers have long been concerned that inadequate organization and coordination exist within the U.S. government to deal with a possible biological or chemical terrorist attack. This issue was discussed in reference to biological attacks in a publication by the Congressional Office of Technology Assessment in 1992, wherein several suggestions for preparing responses were made.[15] In addition, the document presented some issues connected with coordinating interagency activities to prepare responses to chemical and biological terrorist attack. Some obvious suggestions included the development, preparation, and stockpiling of vaccines and antidotes to high-threat agents in strategic locations; more active involvement of experts from the Centers for Disease Control and Public Health Service; development of technologies and systems to provide rapid analysis of chemical and biological agents; and distribution of software expert systems for quick diagnosis of localized outbreaks of disease, so that natural events could be rapidly distinguished from man-made ones.

One important question relates to the balance between mitigating public health consequences and law enforcement priorities. The two do not necessarily work in tandem (the latter effort is led by the Federal Bureau of Investigation and the former by the Federal Emergency Management Agency). Further, while the law enforcement aspect is vital, managing the consequences of a terrorist attack using these weapons of mass destruction must begin as soon as possible. Great care needs to be taken in moving from the first task to the second; to preserve forensic evidence on the one hand and to save as many lives and rescue as many people as possible on the other.

Another important question relates to the role of the military. Surplus protective equipment is available in the military, and several experts have suggested making this available to local responders. An inventory of such surplus should be made quickly to see if this is a viable suggestion, given the need to equip a large number of people. One option would be to work through the states, prioritizing according to perceptions of the threat, and stockpiling such equipment on a state or regional basis. Another possibility would be to work through the National Institute of Justice, which has been assigned a role in disseminating technology, information, and training to local law enforcement authorities. Even though law enforcement officials are not the only emergency responders, there may be a logic in transferring some expertise from the federal level to the local level by this channel.

Doubts about the propriety of the military's involvement in the response to domestic acts of terrorism have hindered such preparations. The Department of Defense possesses a great deal of unique expertise relevant to mitigating the results of an event. But barring action to the contrary by Congress, it is constrained by *posse comitatus* considerations from significantly aiding in the law enforcement aspects of a response to terrorism.

The military may be particularly helpful in addressing the urgent priority for an improvement of the technical means of detecting and identifying chemical agents as soon as possible after an attack. It has a large program to field improved detectors in the wake of the Persian Gulf war. Domestic officials might find such detectors useful for coping with the terrorism problem. It may be useful, for example, to position detectors in likely target areas, if early detection (and proper means of dealing with false alarms) would allow potential victims to take protective action. A sensitive detector might be permanently installed in the air outflow system of a large building, mall, or stadium, and perhaps at transportation centers that might be the target of an attack. Clearly, not all targets can be thus protected, but some can. A sensitive detector (again, with a manageable false alarm rate) might give authorities enough time to take protective action. Military detectors might have to be adapted to the requirements of first responders, who while protected, will have to locate the agents, remove victims from the area, and rapidly discover the type of agent so that appropriate treatment can be given as soon as possible. Detectors will have to be rapid, specific, and sensitive to be most useful.

This points to the need to coordinate programs with the national research laboratories. In this and other response missions, technology does have a role to play. Some efforts have been devoted to developing instrumentation and equipment over the past several years, many through the military research programs and many by the interagency Technical Support Working Group (TSWG). More efforts in research are likely to be productive. Some resources can be made available from within currently existing research programs, especially within the Departments of Defense and Energy. The expansion of TSWG efforts is another option to be considered. Other resources could come from funds authorized (but not yet appropriated) by the Counterterrorism Act of 1996, wherein some $10 million for counterterrorism R&D was allocated to the National Institute of Justice, and various amounts were authorized for counterterrorism purposes (some including R&D) to several agencies, including the FBI. Some of these funds, especially in the case of the FBI, should be devoted to technologies for dealing with chemical and biological terrorism.

It is essential to sustain an effective research and development effort. Apart from medical activities, the real annual R&D spending for responding to chemical or biological terrorism has declined from $53 million to $29 million over the past five years. This suggests that a hard look must be taken at research projects, with a view to removing research that is not particularly productive for counterterrorist purposes.

Although strides in developing interagency coordination have been made over the past few years, at the recent Mirage Gold exercise in New Orleans it became apparent that serious deficiencies exist, indicating the need for significant further work.[16] In fact, the whole problem of responding to CB terrorism is now being actively addressed by the federal government. As an example, the Federal Emergency Management Agency is leading an interagency study on managing and coordinating the federal response to terrorism that employs weapons of mass destruction. As a result of this ongoing and high priority activity, there should be positive developments in 1997 in the effort to develop further the U.S. capacity to deal with this threat. Many U.S. governmental programs are still in their early stages.

Some of the most critical issues of governmental coordination have recently been addressed in a spring 1996 Presidential Decision Directive on terrorism. The precise responsibilities of the many cognizant federal agencies have been clarified and an institutional mechanism for dealing with CB attacks has been established.

## 4. FOLLOW THE COUNTERTERRORISM ACT OF 1996 WITH THE NECESSARY FUNDING AND LEADERSHIP

It is relatively shocking that, following the worst terrorist attack ever in the United States, the Oklahoma City bombing, the Congress took a full year to produce legislation to strengthen the nation's ability to defend itself against the new reality of terrorism within the United States. It is even more shocking that early versions of the legislation paid little attention to the problem of chemical or biological terrorism, in spite of the fact that the Tokyo sarin attack had preceded Oklahoma City by only three weeks. Apparently, congressional and executive branch staff were under such pressure to produce quick legislative prose that they didn't pay attention to a major recent event, possibly because it occurred in another country.

Fortunately, after the year that elapsed and before the legislation finally passed, somewhat more attention was paid to the issue. For example, it will now be easier to charge a miscreant for "only" possessing biological agents. On the other hand, *posse comitatus* arguments prevailed in impeding the U.S. military from taking any investigative role in the area of chemical and biological weapons (although they do have such a role in dealing with nuclear terrorism). This may be unfortunate because the U.S. military possesses unique technical expertise that could be useful. This issue should be revisited so that the role of the military in dealing with criminal acts using weapons of mass destruction is defined consistently among nuclear, chemical, and biological weapons.

The legislation also attempts to address the concern with terrorists who claim political asylum at their port of entry into the United States and then remain in the country for months or years while the matter is being adjudicated. This was done, for example, by Ramzi Yussef, who then, according to authorities, went on to "mastermind" the World Trade Center bombing. Efforts to make this a more difficult practice for future terrorists were partially successful in the new legislation. It remains to be seen how effective the legal changes will be.

Nevertheless, the final passage of the legislation and its signing by President Clinton must be considered as positive, in spite of some problems with civil liberties issues connected with law enforcement powers in parts of the legislation.[17] These issues will probably be revisited in the near future.

For the Act to work, it will require sustained political commitment and money. Both are in doubt. Concerns about political commitment are evident in the turnover of leadership in the Congress and the retirement of a number of key individuals, such as Senator Sam Nunn, who have played a leading role in framing national issues and encouraging federal preparations. And on Capitol Hill, an absence of political commitment always translates into an absence of money. The troubled history of the funding of the HHS emergency preparedness program and the difficult work in summer 1996 of actually appropriating the monies authorized by the Counterterrorism Act demonstrate the uncertain claim of the CB counterterrorism agenda on federal resources.

## CONCLUSION

Recent events have taught the United States some hard truths. It is vulnerable to a variety of terrorist attacks. The terrorist threat to the United States is both domestic and international. Subnational terrorists can use chemical agents with some success. And several domestic individuals associated with extremist groups have shown an interest in acquiring biological weapons. The U.S. government has a responsibility to deal with the problem.

There are good reasons to believe that the United States will suffer terrorist attack with chemical or biological agents within the next few years. But there is not good reason to believe that such an attack would be particularly successful. If the examples provided by the attacks in Tokyo and New York are any guide, terrorist groups seeking to cause mass casualties in the United States may not succeed. They can, however, kill smaller numbers of people. Nor can the possibility of a major success be entirely discounted. Thus serious additional efforts and resources are needed to address this problem.

## NOTES

1.  For a broader list and further discussion, see, for example, U.S. Government, Office of Technology Assessment, *Technology Against Terrorism: The Federal Effort,* OTA-ISC-481 (Washington, DC: U.S. Government Printing Office, September 1991) and U.S. Government, Office of Technology Assessment, *Technology Against Terrorism: Structuring Security,* OTA-ISC- 511, (Washington, DC: U.S. Government Printing Office, January 1992).

2.  These were discussed for biological weapons several years ago by Jeffrey D. Simon in: *Terrorists and the Potential Use of Biological Weapons—A Discussion of Possibilities,* R-3771-AFMIC (Santa Monica, CA: The RAND Corp., December 1989).

3.  U.S. Congress, Office of Technology Assessment, *Technology Against Terrorism: The Federal Effort,* OTA-ISC-481 (Washington, DC: U.S. Government Printing Office, July 1991), p. 22. Also, see testimony of John O'Neill, Federal Bureau of Investigation, before U. S. Senate Permanent Subcommittee on Investigations, Committee on Governmental Affairs, Hearings on Global Proliferation of Weapons of Mass Destruction, October 31-November 1, 1995.

4.  Two titles containing recipes for weapons of mass destruction are *The Poisoner's Handbook* and *Assorted Nasties.* Both these and other interesting literature may be ordered from, for example, Delta Press, a mail order outfit based in Arizona. In one case, even a government agency openly requesting a copy was able to receive these

works within two weeks. The same enterprise also sells Nazi memorabilia, information on "survival" techniques, and advice on how to murder for hire. *The Turner Diaries* is a neo-Nazi tract written under the pseudonym Andrew MacDonald (actually, William Pierce, leader of the National Alliance, a Nazi group based in West Virginia), which glorifies a future fascist insurrection against the U.S. government and denigrates freedom and democracy.

5.   Many individuals from the various defunct Klans have reappeared in leading roles in these "new" movements. Tom Metzger, Stanley McCollum, and Louis Beam are examples, the former having founded "White Aryan Resistance," and the latter two being in the hierarchy of Aryan Nation. See *Klanwatch Intelligence Report*, March 1995, p. 5.

6.   See, for example, testimony of John O'Neill, Hearings on Global Proliferation of Weapons of Mass Destruction, October 31-November 1, 1995.

7.   Many of the right-wing, racist groups that have blossomed in the past few years use "patriot" in their names. This evokes the well-known aphorism of Samuel Johnson to the effect that "patriotism is the last refuge of the scoundrel." It is not surprising or novel, however, that criminal enterprises adopt popular causes or attitudes to cloak their behavior.

8.   See, for example, *Klanwatch Intelligence Report*, October 1995 and John O'Neill, Hearings on Global Proliferation of Weapons of Mass Destruction, October 31-November 1, 1995.

9.   Apparently, there was such evidence in the "Patriot's Council" case, resulting in the first convictions under the Biological Weapons Anti-Terrorism Act of 1989.

10.  A few graduate courses in microbiology appeared to be the extent of his capability; perhaps enough to do mischief, but not enough to do serious research by himself.

11.  J. Kifner, "Man Is Arrested in a Case Involving Deadly Poison," *New York Times*, December 23, 1995, p.7. *The Poisoner's Handbook* was among those books (see note 4).

12.  Again, see note 4.

13.  Details on these contacts have been in innumerable press articles. The call by McVeigh to a neo-Nazi German national working on "security" (who has since fled the country) at Elohim City has been confirmed both by McVeigh and the Identity group. For some details, see *Klanwatch Intelligence Report*, October 1995, p. 2.

14.  "New Charges Filed Against Alleged Leader of Bombing," *Washington Post*, October 7, 1995, p. A14.

15.  U.S. Government, Office of Technology Assessment, *Technology Against Terrorism: Structuring Security*, January 1992, pp. 35-44 and pp. 49-50.

16.  Minority Staff Statement of the U.S. Senate Permanent Subcommittee on Investigations, Committee on Governmental Affairs, "Hearings on Global Proliferation of Weapons of Mass Destruction: Response to Domestic Terrorism", March 27, 1996, pp. 13-17.

17.  I exclude discussion of the modifications in habeas corpus requirements for death row appeals, which were appended to the legislation. These have a minimal relationship to terrorism, being, rather, aimed at common criminal cases. There are many diverse opinions on this issue, and I consider it unfortunate that this language was included in the legislation, because it muddies the waters considerably in discussions of the merits of the rest of the Act.

# Policy Approaches to Chemical and Biological Terrorism

## Jonathan B. Tucker

The March 1995 sarin attack on the Tokyo subway system by members of Aum Shinrikyo, a fanatical Buddhist cult, was a wake-up call for policymakers the world over.[1] This incident demonstrated that despite the technical hurdles involved in the manufacture of chemical and biological (CB) weapons, determined terrorists can gain access to the production equipment, raw materials, and scientific expertise needed to produce them.

Another grim lesson of the Tokyo subway incident was that urban populations are extremely vulnerable to even small quantities of chemical or biological agents. Although 12 people died and more than 5,000 were injured as a consequence of the Tokyo attack, the toll would have been far higher had it not been for the poor quality of the nerve agent (which had been synthesized hastily the day before and diluted with solvent) and the crude delivery system (plastic bags filled with liquid agent, which were punctured with sharpened umbrella tips). If the Aum terrorists had disseminated an aerosol of high-grade sarin in the crowded subway system, the Tokyo attack could have easily inflicted tens of thousands of casualties.

Terrorist use of CB agents in urban areas not only has the potential to kill and injure masses of people but could enable small numbers of extremists to disrupt society on an unprecedented scale. Despite the relatively few deaths and serious injuries from the Tokyo subway incident, the attack had a devastating psychological impact, triggering widespread panic and anxiety and undermining the credibility of the Japanese government.

Democratic societies are particularly vulnerable to CB terrorism. Whereas authoritarian states can crush terrorist groups operating on their territory through the massive use of surveillance and repression, liberal democracies deliberately limit the power of the state and tolerate subversive and even hateful speech. Since it would be self-defeating for democratic societies to bolster domestic security at the expense of civil liberties, policymakers must find the right balance between individual liberty and social regulation. Without banning fringe groups or depriving them of their constitutional rights, government authorities must be prepared to intervene promptly to prevent actions that threaten public health and safety.

## Likelihood of Future Attacks

Although the small number of cases of CB terrorism to date makes it difficult to extrapolate the probability of similar incidents in the future, policymakers cannot afford to be complacent. Much like a nuclear reactor accident, a CB terrorist attack is a "low probability, high consequence event" that warrants careful government planning and preparation.

In the future, terrorist groups motivated by religious fanaticism or extremist ideology might be drawn to CB weapons as a means to inflict mass casualties, disrupt society, or undermine government authority. The most dangerous terrorists are those who believe that violence directed at a particular racial group or category of people (e.g., federal officials) is legitimate or even divinely sanctioned. According to one analyst, "Whereas secular terrorists generally consider indiscriminate violence immoral and counterproductive, religious terrorists regard such violence not only as morally justified, but as a necessary expedient for the attainment of their goals."[2] Some terrorism experts worry that as the year 2000 approaches, "millennial" religious cults with a belief in apocalyptic prophecy could also resort to use of mass-casualty weapons.[3]

Terrorist groups seeking to acquire chemical or biological weapons could either produce them on their own or attempt to buy or steal existing munitions. Aum Shinrikyo has shown that the production option is feasible, and there is growing concern about theft or purchase. According to an October 1995 report by the Henry L. Stimson Center, Russian chemical weapons (CW) stockpiles are inadequately secured in aging facilities guarded by poorly paid soldiers. Security is problematic at four of the seven CW storage sites in Russia, including poor lighting, gaps in fencing, wooden storage buildings with padlocked doors, few guards at the main entry and exit points, and a lack of computerized inventory control systems. The Stimson Center report concludes: "Russian chemical weapons storage facilities appear to be vulnerable to theft from within and attack from without."[4]

Since corruption flourishes in contemporary Russia, including the military, poorly paid guards might be tempted to steal chemical munitions and sell them to terrorists. Chemical artillery shells are portable and far easier for a terrorist to use than a nuclear weapon. As for biological weapons (BW), freeze-dried microbial and toxin agents are extremely potent per unit weight and easily concealed in small containers that could be smuggled across borders or through airport security systems.

Another issue of concern is the potential for "brain-drain" of chemical and biological weapon (CBW) specialists from Russia to other countries, including states that sponsor terrorism. Because of the decline of the military-industrial complex in the former Soviet Union, many CBW experts no longer have sufficient income to support their families and may be susceptible to lucrative employment offers from proliferant states or terrorist groups. According to U.S. Senate testimony by Dr. Vil Mirzayanov, a former Russian military chemist turned whistleblower, "In my opinion, we were all very lucky that the notorious gas attack in the Tokyo subway was prepared and carried out by dilettantes. Had true professionals from Russia executed it, using military-strength sarin, there would have been a real catastrophe."[5]

## GROWING U.S. GOVERNMENT CONCERN

The Tokyo sarin attack has forced senior U.S. officials to address the frightening potential of CB terrorism. On March 20, 1996, the first anniversary of the subway incident, Director of Central Intelligence John M. Deutch told a U.S. Senate hearing that the risk of an attack by a terrorist group armed with chemical weapons was significantly greater than that posed by the threat of "loose nukes" or black market nuclear weapons technology.[6] A week later, Gordon Oehler, director of the Central Intelligence Agency's Nonproliferation Center, testified, "Extremist groups worldwide are increasingly learning how to manufacture chemical and biological agents, and the potential for additional chemical and biological attacks by such groups continues to grow."[7]

Reflecting heightened U.S. government awareness of the CB terrorist threat, security preparations for the 1996 Summer Olympic Games in Atlanta included secret exercises by the Federal Bureau of Investigation (FBI) and other agencies designed to simulate a CB attack and cope with the mayhem it might produce.[8] One exercise, codenamed "Olympic Charlie," involved the hypothetical release of the persistent nerve agent VX.[9]

Although the vulnerability of urban centers to CB terrorism is a frightening reality for which there are no easy technical fixes, policymakers should neither throw up their hands in despair nor adopt an attitude of complacency but should take practical measures to contain the problem. In the case of the Tokyo subway incident, improved intelligence, surveillance, and early police intervention against Aum Shinrikyo could have helped to prevent or mitigate the attack. An effective CB counterterrorism strategy would combine two complementary approaches: preemption and civil defense. Measures to support both tracks are discussed in the following sections.

# Preemption

Preemption, or the ability to prevent CB terrorist attacks before they occur, presupposes the ability to detect such activities at an early stage. Possible indicators include statements or publications by extremist groups that hint at the intent to resort to violence, the acquisition of CB precursor materials and equipment, or the production and testing of toxic agents. Although the Aum Shinrikyo cult engaged in all of these activities, in some cases rather blatantly, the Japanese government failed to intervene in time to prevent a tragic loss of life. Policy options that would support a strategy of preemption are discussed below.

***Improve interagency coordination in developing CB counterterrorism policy.*** A major obstacle to the development of effective CB counterterrorism policies has been a lack of effective coordination within the U.S. government. Since the issue of terrorism is multidimensional, involving aspects of technology, national security, intelligence, law enforcement, and public health, it cuts across the interests of several executive departments and agencies. As a result, federal officials have addressed the problem in a piecemeal manner, producing a national response plan that is scattered and unfocused. The fact that Congress is organized to authorize and appropriate money for specific agencies rather than to address cross-cutting issues such as CB terrorism has exacerbated the difficulty of interagency coordination within the executive branch.

Another bureaucratic hurdle is the fact that under current U.S. law, the CIA is restricted to monitoring international terrorist groups overseas while the FBI has the lead role in tracking their activities on U.S. territory. Since these two rival agencies are not prone to share information freely, the result may be a major disconnect between foreign and domestic intelligence collection on key terrorist organizations. In the absence of effective coordination, this division of labor has become dangerously anachronistic.

To overcome "turf battles" among the various intelligence and policy agencies within the executive branch that have a stake in NBC counterterrorism policy, the president should establish a centralized coordinating mechanism under the auspices of the National Security Advisor. Congress should also improve the coherence of the legislative and appropriations process in the NBC counterterrorism field by establishing select committees of the House and Senate with jurisdiction over all facets of the issue.

***Refocus intelligence collection on unconventional terrorist threats.*** A strategy of preemption requires good intelligence on terrorist groups, both domestic and international. Before the Tokyo subway attack, the U.S. government knew little about Aum Shinrikyo, despite the cult's worldwide efforts to acquire CB agent precursors and production equipment through a network of legitimate and front companies.[10] During U.S. Senate hearings in November 1995 on the Tokyo subway incident, senior counterterrorism officials from the FBI, the CIA, and the Department of Defense admitted that they had focused their intelligence-gathering efforts on state-sponsored terrorists or those with a political agenda, and thus had not targeted Aum Shinrikyo prior to the Tokyo attack.[11]

In future, the U.S. intelligence community should allocate greater resources to monitoring "unconventional" fringe groups such as religious cults, survivalist militias, and supremacist organizations that appear capable of large-scale violence. This expanded collection effort should also include intelligence-sharing with friendly countries (including Russia) on international terrorist groups that might be contemplating CB attacks. Of course, exhortations to improve intelligence gathering are easier said than done. Since most production equipment for CB agents has legitimate commercial uses, and the small quantities of agent needed for terrorist purposes are easy to conceal, there are few telltale "signatures" associated with such activities. Accordingly, detection relies primarily on human-source information (infiltrators and defectors) rather than "national technical means" such as reconnaissance satellites.

The government should never use domestic counterterrorism as an excuse to suppress the civil liberties of groups that espouse unpopular views but do not resort to violence. Nevertheless, if the FBI has "probable cause" to believe that extremists are seeking CB-related materials with an intent to use them for terrorist purposes, the bureau should obtain a warrant to engage in intensive surveillance, including wiretaps and infiltration by undercover agents. Despite the difficulty of penetrating extremist groups, such tactics may provide the only way to obtain the strategic warning needed to prevent, or at least mitigate, a CB terrorist attack.

***Pass domestic legislation outlawing CB weapons.*** A fundamental prerequisite for a strategy of preemption is the existence of domestic laws making the development, production, possession, and use of CB agents a serious crime. Such legislation provides the basis for aggressive enforcement activity, including preemptive police raids and arrests when there is probable cause to believe that groups have acquired CB-related materials for criminal purposes.

The 1972 Biological and Toxin Weapons Convention (BWC), which bans the development, production, and stockpiling of biological and toxin weapons, requires parties to take "any necessary measures" to implement the treaty. Even so, it was not until more than 15 years after the BWC was signed that the U.S. Congress finally passed domestic implementing legislation, the Biological Weapons Anti-Terrorism Act of 1989. This law makes the prohibitions of the BWC binding on all citizens and businesses on the territory of the United States and on U.S. nationals residing overseas, and imposes punitive sanctions for violations. To date, however, only about 40 of the 135 states parties have passed similar domestic legislation.

With respect to chemical weapons, current U.S. domestic law prohibits use but not acquisition or possession. The 1993 Chemical Weapons Convention (CWC), which is expected to enter into force in early 1997, requires states parties to pass implementing legislation making it a crime for any individual or business under each country's jurisdiction to develop, produce, stockpile, or use chemical weapons. Until such legislation is passed, however, it is not technically illegal for anyone in the United States to produce or otherwise acquire chemical weapons—provided there is no conspiracy to use them for criminal purposes.

Although the CWC cannot prevent chemical terrorism, it will reinforce the international norm against the acquisition and use of chemical weapons. The convention will also require member states to report the activities of companies that produce, process, consume, import, or export chemical weapon precursors, obliging both governments and private companies to be more vigilant about suspicious transactions. The implementing legislation mandated by the CWC will create additional obstacles for terrorists by requiring states parties to criminalize the production, acquisition, stockpiling, or smuggling of CW agents and certain precursors by individuals or businesses. As a result, the legislation should enable law enforcement personnel to intervene early against terrorists seeking to acquire chemical weapons before an attack actually occurs. Companies that knowingly assist terrorists to acquire chemical weapons will also be liable to punitive sanctions. In view of these benefits, it is not surprising that the Japanese government's first policy response to the Tokyo subway incident was to ratify the Chemical Weapons Convention and pass domestic implementing legislation.

***Enhance vigilance during international crises.*** A strategy of preemption requires heightened vigilance with respect to external terrorist threats, particularly in wartime or during periods of increased international tension. Throughout the Persian Gulf crisis of 1990-91, for example, the FBI, CIA, Department of Defense (DOD), and Immigration and Naturalization Service (INS) were placed on a war footing and took enhanced external and internal security measures to protect American domestic and overseas targets from Iraqi terrorism. According to press reports, U.S. intelligence agencies foiled operations by about 30 Iraqi-sponsored terrorist teams while they were still outside the United States.[12] As an additional line of defense, the United States should train law enforcement and customs personnel in countries with notoriously lax border controls, such as the Newly Independent States of the former Soviet Union.

***Promote international cooperation on counterterrorism.*** The United States and other like-minded countries should negotiate an international treaty committing them to share intelligence on terrorist groups, cooperate in tracking down perpetrators, interdict illegal shipments of CB agent precursors and production equipment, authorize the hot pursuit of fugitives across international borders, and establish clear-cut and workable extradition agreements for captured terrorists.

***Expand assistance to Russia for chemical and biological disarmament.*** Since terrorists could acquire chemical weapons by sale or theft, particularly from Russia's vast yet poorly secured CW stockpile, the United States and its allies should provide additional technical and financial assistance to facilitate the destruction of Russian chemical weapons and improve their physical security in the interim. It is also essential to prevent a "brain drain" of Russian chemical and biological weapons experts to rogue states and terrorist organizations by increasing the share of funding at the International Science and Technology Center (ISTC) in Moscow for civilian research projects employing former military chemists and biologists. As of December 1995, only 3 percent of ISTC funding was allocated to former CB weapons specialists, compared with 63 percent to former nuclear weapons scientists and 16 percent to former missile experts.[13]

***Promote self-policing by U.S. companies.*** The U.S. Department of Commerce should expand its efforts to educate chemical companies and biological suppliers about the threat of CB terrorism and urge them to police themselves more effectively. At present, companies are not required to investigate the *bona fides* of prospective customers, and once an export license has been approved, they are under no obligation to verify the declared end-use of a dual-capable product. As a result of this lax attitude, Aum Shinrikyo was able to purchase on the open market all of the ingredients and equipment it needed to produce two deadly nerve agents, sarin and VX. According to the U.S. Senate staff report on the Tokyo subway incident, however, "some of the items sought by the Aum were not delivered because U.S. company representatives were suspicious of the Aum and its purported end use of the product. This is a good example of self-policing by the private sector, and efforts to sensitize industry to their responsibility should be promoted."[14]

A self-policing system for industry, in which suppliers of CB precursors and production equipment assume at least partial responsibility for preventing the misuse of their products, would be more desirable than adding yet another layer of government regulation. Under such a system, companies would be required to do some basic background research on new clients to make sure they are legitimate, and to confirm that shipped products had actually been delivered and used for the intended purpose. In the event suspicious activities were observed, suppliers would be required to report them to the appropriate government authorities.

In much the same way, commercial laboratories that supply seed cultures of infectious pathogens for biomedical and public-health research should screen their customers to make sure they have a legitimate need for these hazardous materials before being allowed to purchase them. Such restrictions would make it harder for terrorists to obtain deadly microbial and toxin agents by impersonating biomedical scientists or by submitting orders on stolen or fictitious university letterhead. Indeed, a member of the white supremacist organization Aryan Nation was arrested in 1995 for attempting to purchase a freeze-dried sample of bubonic plague from a Maryland biological supply house.[15] The Antiterrorism and Effective Death Penalty Act, signed into law in April 1996, mandates the executive branch to establish a licensing procedure that balances the legitimate need of biomedical research scientists for access to pathogenic microorganisms and toxins against the imperative to prevent these deadly materials from falling into the wrong hands.

**Provide antiterrorism training to local police.** The FBI, with technical assistance from the Department of Defense, should train large urban police departments in specialized surveillance, forensic, and law enforcement techniques related to CB terrorism. This program would entail training detectives and officers to recognize criminal behavior on the part of religious cults and extremist organizations, as well as subtle indicators of CB agent acquisition, development, and production. Examples of possible indicators include the theft or purchase of biological cultures, precursor chemicals, and dual-capable production equipment from university laboratories or commercial suppliers.

# CIVIL DEFENSE

Although a strategy of preemption would aim to uncover and take action against terrorists before they strike, there is no sure-fire way of preventing such attacks. For this reason, responsible governments must also take measures to mitigate the effects of a CB terrorist incident should it occur. Whereas countries such as Sweden, Switzerland, and Israel have long incorporated civil defense into their overall defense concept, the United States has emphasized protecting soldiers from the battlefield use of CB weapons while neglecting the development of effective civil defenses against urban terrorist attacks.

The public health consequences of a chemical weapons attack would depend on its location, the type of agent employed, the delivery system, and the prevailing atmospheric conditions. An insidious characteristic of chemical weapons that differentiates them from conventional explosives is the risk of secondary exposure from buildings and people contaminated with a persistent agent, which could claim additional victims up to several hours after the initial attack. To prevent such a multiplier effect, casualties and buildings would have to be monitored and promptly decontaminated, greatly increasing the number of people needed to manage the disaster.

A covert biological weapons attack would be even harder to manage medically because of its delayed effects. The exposed population would not experience the onset of symptoms until after an incubation period lasting a few days, by which time the affected individuals could have dispersed widely. An effective surveillance mechanism would have to be in place to detect the disease outbreak and differentiate it from a natural epidemic. Since it would not be possible to vaccinate civilian populations prior to a terrorist BW attack, the medical response would have to rely on post-exposure treatment with antibiotics and antisera. Given the speed at which pathogens such as anthrax can induce a life-threatening illness, however, rapid identification of the agent would be essential to save lives through antimicrobial therapy.

An effective CB counterterrorism strategy must include the capability for rapid emergency response to a terrorist attack, which could occur without advance warning. To narrow the scope of the problem, civil defenses against CB terrorism should be based on "most likely" rather than "worst case" scenarios. Accordingly, protective measures should be focused on the targets of highest risk, such as government buildings, and enclosed public spaces, such as lobbies, airports, and subways.

Much remains to be done to enhance the ability of federal, state, and local governments to respond effectively to CB terrorist incidents. Special requirements associated with the medical response to CB terrorism include: (1) rapid identification of the toxic or infectious agents; (2) tracking of the agent cloud to identify contaminated and safe areas; (3) establishment of initial holding areas to decontaminate victims prior to treatment, where medical personnel would work in full protective gear; (4) standardization of treatment, including medical equipment and drugs; (5) acquisition of supplies and procedures for the prompt administration of antidotes or antibiotics to a large number of victims; (6) rapid and logical triage of victims according to severity of injury, followed by matching of seriously ill patients to appropriate tertiary care facilities; and (7) decontamination of victims, buildings, and equipment.[16]

A capability for emergency response and consequence management of a CB terrorist incident would entail some or all of the following policy options:

***Improve coordination of federal emergency response planning with state and local authorities.*** Although the federal government has an interagency working group on nuclear, biological, and chemical (NBC) terrorism, and major cities such as New York and Los Angeles have developed their own contingency plans, there has been relatively little coordination between the federal and local levels. Part of the problem derives from statutory restrictions on agency powers. For example, although current law authorizes the Federal Emergency Management Agency (FEMA) to advise states and localities on emergency planning, it has no authority to dictate such planning activities or their content.

To set a national agenda for action, Congress should authorize the FBI, FEMA, and other responsible federal agencies to develop a comprehensive national civil defense plan that specifies how emergency response and public health resources at the federal, state, and local levels would be mobilized to deal with CB terrorist incidents. After the national plan has been developed, civil defense officials should conduct annual or semiannual exercises in which they simulate a CB terrorist attack and test out emergency responses under realistic field conditions.

**Establish emergency medical response teams in urban areas.** In the aftermath of the Tokyo subway incident, the National Security Council asked the U.S. Public Health Service to develop a contingency plan to minimize casualties and contain contamination following a CB terrorist attack. This plan calls for the creation, under the auspices of the National Disaster Medical System, of special "metropolitan medical strike teams" who would be on call 24 hours a day and capable of responding within 30 to 90 minutes of a terrorist incident. In June 1996, the U.S. Public Health Service established a model metropolitan strike team in Washington, D.C., consisting of 42 volunteers with backgrounds in emergency preparedness, law enforcement, and medicine.[17] Similar teams should be established in other major U.S. cities.

**Establish a federal chemical and biological emergency response unit.** On June 1, 1996, the U.S. Marine Corps activated a new Chemical and Biological Incident Response Force, whose primary mission is to manage the consequences of CB terrorist attacks at Navy and State Department installations overseas.[18] In addition, legislation introduced in June 1996 by U.S. Senators Sam Nunn, Richard Lugar, and Pete Domenici, and subsequently passed by both houses of Congress, mandates the Department of Defense to develop and maintain a Chemical/Biological Emergency Response Team (CBERT), which would be deployed in the event of a domestic CB terrorist incident. According to the legislation, the CBERT will be "composed of members of the armed forces and employees of the Department of Defense who are capable of aiding federal, state, and local officials in the detection, neutralization, containment, dismantlement, and disposal of weapons of mass destruction containing chemical, biological, or related materials."[19]

**Stockpile CB defensive materials in large urban areas.** FEMA should purchase and stockpile CB defensive materials at major medical centers in the 20 largest U.S. cities. Such stockpiles might include CB agent monitoring devices, antidotes against chemical nerve agents, and antibiotics and antisera. Logistical procedures should also be developed and exercised so that the proper antidotes, together with the means to deliver them to large numbers of people, are prepositioned at a few central locations (e.g., large medical centers and police stations) so they could be transported rapidly to the scene of a CB terrorist attack. Items of protective equipment developed for the military, such as antidote autoinjectors, must also be modified to make them suitable for civilian use. While it would be impractical to distribute large numbers of gas masks to civilian populations, emergency response and medical teams will require full protective gear.

**Develop public service announcements for emergency broadcast.** FEMA and the U.S. Public Health Service should develop public service announcements (PSAs) for emergency radio and TV broadcasts in the event of a CB attack. These PSAs would inform people in the affected area about the nature of the attack and how to protect themselves from contamination, thereby reducing secondary casualties and suppressing widespread panic.

**Upgrade CB detection and identification devices.** Although field detection systems should be capable of identifying CB agents in close to "real time" with a low probability of false negatives or false positives, this goal remains elusive. Congress should therefore continue to increase funding for research and development of improved CB agent detection and identification systems, and encourage joint development efforts with allied countries. DOD should also transfer leading edge CB detection technologies to local law enforcement authorities soon after they have been developed for military use. In some cases, it may be necessary to modify the military detectors to make them more user-friendly or to avoid divulging classified information.

***Expand epidemiological surveillance programs.*** Congress should appropriate funds to expand the epidemiological surveillance programs operated by the U.S. Centers for Disease Control under the auspices of the World Health Organization. While offering broad benefits for international health, this mechanism would help to distinguish covert BW attacks from unusual outbreaks of infectious disease resulting from natural causes.[20]

***Promote the development of new antidotes and therapeutic drugs.*** Congress should provide incentives for the pharmaceutical industry to develop broad-spectrum antibacterial and antiviral drugs capable of treating exposures to a variety of putative BW agents. Because the high cost and uncertainty associated with the development of such drugs deter many pharmaceutical companies from pursuing them, government tax incentives are warranted. In addition to the potential use of such new medications in treating BW agent exposures, they would be of great value against naturally occurring infectious diseases, which have increasingly become resistant to standard antibiotics.

# CONCLUSIONS

Although another large-scale incident of CB terrorism remains unlikely, the potentially devastating impact of such an attack in civilian casualties and psychological trauma warrants a major national investment in counterterrorist activities. Although there is no simple technical means to reduce the vulnerability of urban populations to CB terrorism, the two-pronged strategy presented above—combining measures for pre-emptive action with emergency response and consequence management—offers practical steps for mitigating this emerging threat.

Given the reality of finite government resources, some prioritization of investments and policy measures will be required. Since prevention is better than cure, the primary emphasis should be on improvements in intelligence collection, surveillance, interdiction, and other preemptive measures. Nevertheless, a well-coordinated system for emergency response and consequence management will also be essential in the event preemption fails.

## NOTES

1.  This chapter draws extensively on a longer treatment of the same subject, "Chemical/Biological Terrorism: Coping with a New Threat," *Politics and the Life Sciences* 15 (2), September 1996.

2.  Bruce Hoffman, "Holy Terror: The Implications of Terrorism Motivated by a Religious Imperative," Report No. P-7834 (Santa Monica, CA: RAND Corporation, 1993), p. 2.

3.  T. Post, "Doomsday Cults: 'Only the Beginning'," *Newsweek* 125 (April 3, 1995), p. 40.

4.  Amy E. Smithson, "Improving the Security of Russia's Chemical Weapons Stockpile," in Amy E. Smithson et al, *Chemical Weapons Disarmament in Russia: Problems and Prospects*, Report No. 17 (Washington, D.C.: Henry L. Stimson Center, October 1995), p. 19.

5.  Vil S. Mirzayanov, Statement before the U.S. Senate Permanent Subcommittee on Investigations, Committee on Governmental Affairs, Hearing on Global Proliferation of Weapons of Mass Destruction, November 1, 1995.

6.  Tim Weiner, "U.S. Is Called Vulnerable to Terrorist Chemical Arms," *New York Times*, March 21, 1996, p. A4.

7.  Robert Green, "Nuclear, Chemical Terror Threat is High, CIA Says," Reuters News Service, March 27, 1996.

8.  R. Jeffrey Smith, "U.S. on Alert for Terrorism at the Olympics," *International Herald Tribune*, April 24, 1996, p. 3.

9.  Douglas Pasternak, "Let the Games Begin," *U.S. News & World Report,* vol. 120, no. 25 (June 24, 1996), p. 58.

10. R. Jeffrey Smith, "Japanese Cult Had Network of Front Companies, Investigators Say," *Washington Post*, November 1, 1995, p. A8; Christopher Drew, "Japanese Sect Tried to Buy U.S. Arms Technology, Senator Says," *New York Times*, October 31, 1995, p. A5.

11. R. Jeffrey Smith, "Senators Scold Spy Agencies Over Cult," *Washington Post*, November 2, 1995, p. A15.

12. Michael Wines, "International Teamwork May Have Foiled Terror," *New York Times,* March 4, 1991, p. A11.

13. International Science and Technology Center (Moscow), Second Annual Report: January-December 1995, "Weapons Background of Experts Participating in ISTC Projects" [pie chart], p. 6.

14. U.S. Senate Permanent Subcommittee on Investigations, Committee on Governmental Affairs, "Staff Statement, Hearings on Global Proliferation of Weapons of Mass Destruction: A Case Study on Aum Shinrikyo," mimeo, October 31, 1995, p. 76.

15. Julian Perry Robinson, "News Chronology: May through August 1995," *Chemical Weapons Convention Bulletin* 29 (September 1995), p. 19.

16. J. Shemer and Y.L. Danon, "Eighty Years of the Threat and Use of Chemical Warfare: The Medico-Organizational Challenge," in: *Chemical Warfare Medicine: Aspects and Perspectives from the Persian Gulf War*, Y.L Danon and J. Shemer, eds., (Jerusalem: Gefen Publishing House, 1994).

17. Douglas Pasternak with Jennifer Seter, "Planning for the Worst," *U.S. News and World Report*, June 24, 1996, p. 61.

18. Lois R. Ember, "Marines Offer Rapid Response to Chemical/Biological Terrorism," *Chemical and Engineering News*, July 1, 1996, pp. 22-23.

19. "Title XIV: Defense Against Weapons of Mass Destruction, Sect. 1414: Chemical-Biological Emergency Response Team," *Congressional Record-House*, July 30, 1996, p. H9074.

20. Mark L. Wheelis, "Strengthening the Biological Weapons Convention through Global Epidemiological Surveillance," *Politics and the Life Sciences* 11 (August 1992):179-189.

# The Essential Tasks of Emergency Preparedness

## Frank Young

The threat of terrorism with weapons of mass destruction is real. While the first line of defense is good defense and effective crisis management, the nation must be prepared for the unthinkable in terms of health and medical consequences. Because it is likely that both local and state resources would be overwhelmed in the aftermath of a terrorist attack with weapons of mass destruction, an integrated local, state, and federal response is required. As a physician who has addressed these issues in the laboratory, as a former government official managing the public health response to terrorism due to chemical poisonings with cyanide, and as the leader of the health and medical consequence response in the Federal Response Plan (FRP) under the coordination of the Federal Emergency Management Agency (FEMA), I have been forced to wrestle with the need for an integrated response from both a technical and a policy perspective. I am grateful for this opportunity in the very last days of my government service to offer a number of key lessons for the work ahead. I identify five such lessons:

*Lesson one*. Chemical terrorism is not a fundamentally new problem. During the last couple of decades there have been many attempts to use chemical poisons, especially cyanide, for the purpose of extortion, murder, or the extraction of political concessions. I am familiar with more than 100 threats to poison, or real or attempted poisonings. These experiences have taught the public health system the necessity of preparing for such acts of terrorism. The question before us is whether or how to calibrate this system in the light of new requirements. We need not start from scratch.

**Lesson two.** The ability to predict acts of domestic terrorism with chemical or biological agents is low. On the other hand, the likelihood of domestic terrorism is probably growing. The United States, as the dominant power in the world today and as primary defender of an international status quo, stands out as a major target of terrorist attack. The dominant role of the media in our society fuels the hope of terrorists that individual acts will make political statements heard by many. Indeed, the unfortunate and ill-advised media feeding frenzy seen in response to so many recent acts of terrorism is likely only to encourage further violence. Moreover, access to the Internet and other resources makes it relatively easy for terrorists to learn how to make chemical or biological agents, and empowers individuals motivated by particularly human passions, releasing them from dependence on state sponsors.

**Lesson three.** Whereas predictability is low, vulnerability is enormous—even to rare events. We do not live in a police state and we hope we never will. But there are many potential points of terrorist attack in our open and highly complex society and a successful attack could be crippling.

**Lesson four.** Different weapons of mass destruction pose different problems. An improvised nuclear device mixed with explosives has the potential to cause large numbers of casualties and radiological contamination. A chemical weapon could kill many people if delivered with the necessary efficiency in the type of setting conducive to a successful attack. Both chemical and nuclear devices produce casualties immediately. A biological agent is more insidious and could cause major panic. Fortunately, we have an excellent epidemiological and treatment system for infectious agents in the United States. However horrendous these weapons are, we should not forget that the traditional instruments of terrorism—guns and bombs—are perfectly effective at killing indiscriminately and in large numbers. Each puts very different requirements on the public health system.

**Lesson five.** Medical preparedness is the final line of defense. In the United States, we can rightly be proud of our medical system's capacity to respond to emergency public health requirements. But the emergency system overall is geared to respond to small numbers of people injured primarily due to trauma, including transportation accidents, medical emergencies such as heart attacks, and localized cases of violence. The responses to these types of emergencies are not as relevant to injury caused by chemical and biological attack.

## PUBLIC HEALTH CONCERNS

The primary public health concerns associated with chemical and biological terrorism include but are not limited to: public health advisories, agent identification, hazard identification, clinical medical support, pharmacy support, worker safety, and mortuary support.

In the event of a chemical attack with a highly lethal agent, immediate therapy is essential. It is important to emphasize that the March 1995 terrorist attack in Japan was not with a highly lethal concentration of sarin; only those in the immediate vicinity of the release were killed. Thus, the threat to health and safety for both the first responders and many of the victims was relatively low. Nonetheless, even in a situation where a relatively small number of people are killed, as was the case when cyanide was found in Tylenol, public panic demands a prompt response. First responders have informed us that proper equipment and training are essential to ensure a prompt response and, moreover, that some metropolitan areas are currently unprepared. These courageous fire fighters, police, and emergency medical support personnel risk their lives to protect U.S. citizens. It is just wrong to ask them to respond without proper preparation.

With a biological agent, there is an incubation period followed by a sudden onset of symptoms. The rapid identification of the agent is necessary to save lives through antimicrobial therapy as the organism can spread to individuals outside the original site of attack. Since public anxiety can be expected, accurate public health advisories, an appropriate supply of medicine, and the capacity to respond medically are among the most essential actions.

At this time, there is a weakly-coordinated public health infrastructure to deal with the medical consequences of such acts of terrorism. The most glaring deficiencies are the following: (1) there is episodic, limited integration at the local, state, and federal levels of the various disciplines required to respond to this type of threat; (2) at all levels there are inadequate numbers of trained and experienced responders; (3) in high risk metropolitan areas medical responses are not in place; (4) the infrastructure to respond to the increasing number of emergencies is inadequate, especially secure communications; and (5) there are significant gaps in the early warning and detection systems, identification of chemical and biological agents, surveillance, decontamination procedures, and worker safety. The medical strike team approach piloted by the Metropolitan Washington Council of Governments is designed to enhance the capacity of a metropolitan region to respond to terrorist attack.

# Crisis and Consequence Management

The foregoing review of deficiencies *could* suggest that the United States is totally unprepared for the kinds of terrorism analyzed here. This is not true. In fact, a good deal of attention has been given to the subject, as well as a good deal of planning, as I argued in testimony delivered to the U.S. Senate's Permanent Subcommittee on Investigations, Committee on Governmental Affairs, on November 1, 1995. It is important to keep this planning in mind when determining where to focus future resources and efforts.

The federal management of domestic crises is the responsibility of the Federal Bureau of Investigation (FBI), with FEMA and the other domestic departments and agencies working closely to support the FBI through their crisis management plan. In the event of a terrorist attack, the Department of Health and Human Services (HHS) provides technical assistance in threat assessment and emergency consultation. The individuals who provide this assistance must be accessible for consultation within an hour of the request. HHS will also rapidly deploy individuals to supplement the FBI for on-site technical assistance. These experts are prepared to deal with consequence management if the need arises. It is important to note that training and exercises are required to ensure that roles are clearly known and the transition from crisis to consequence management occurs smoothly.

FEMA is responsible for consequence management under the Federal Response Plan, which establishes primary responsibilities for the various emergency support functions. The plan enlists support from 26 departments and agencies. When the resources of the local and state governments are exhausted, and the president approves a governor's request for a federal disaster declaration, FEMA activates the FRP and tasks the primary departments and agencies to provide essential services through formal mission assignments.

An essential element in the response to any disaster, whether natural or man-made, is the National Disaster Medical System (NDMS). This system is made up of four departments and agencies, with HHS in the lead, and includes FEMA, the Department of Defense, and the Department of Veterans Affairs. The NDMS has three major components: patient care, patient evacuation, and patient in-hospital care. Currently, there are 60 disaster medical assistance teams in existence, of which 21 can mobilize within 6 hours, with supplies and equipment for 72 hours of operation.

In any such disaster, the key to effective response is speed. The number of lives lost will, in large measure, be a direct result of the rapidity of the immediate response capabilities. Weapons of mass destruction cause death, injury, and environmental destruction. Because loss of life is the paramount concern, the immediate and initial focus on the impact of terrorism must be on the health and medical consequences and the capacity of the first responders to save lives.

Immediately after the Tokyo subway attack, the Public Health Service was tasked to develop a plan of operation for the health and medical consequences of chemical and biologic terrorism. Funds were allocated for initial planning purposes. The Office of Emergency Preparedness, as the lead office in HHS, serves as chair and FEMA as the cochair of the interagency committee to develop the immediate health and medical response to terrorism with biologic and chemical agents. The committee developed an interim plan that integrates the immediate health and medical responses of the federal agencies in support of states and local governments.

The plan has many elements. Of particular note are the following: (1) it calls for an assessment of gaps in response capability; (2) it notes that planning, training, and exercises are essential to prepare first responders; (3) first responders need the support of special metropolitan strike teams that are trained and ready to cope with chemical and biologic agents. Such teams should be prepared to respond within 30 to 90 minutes in high-risk metropolitan areas; (4) communication equipment and expertise are likely to be among the weakest links in any response to a terrorist incident. In the aftermath of the New York Trade Center and Oklahoma City bombings, communications capacity was limited for about three hours; and (5) it is important to review the allocation of resources and priorities within the NDMS to determine how they should be shifted from a primary focus on natural disasters to a more balanced focus on both natural and man-made disasters, especially in large metropolitan areas.

With sufficient funding, HHS could support the following priorities: (1) initiation and coordination of integrated planning and evaluation activities with local, state, and federal authorities; (2) training of health professionals, emergency responders, and emergency managers at all three levels, to augment the skills of personnel involved in medical response, early detection, surveillance, inspection, sample transportation, and laboratory detection; (3) improvement of medical response coordination through additional medical, scientific, and logistic personnel, who would provide technical assistance, procure required antidotes and antibiotics, and establish the medical support unit to coordinate the emergency response; (4) enhancement of warning and detection systems to reduce the severe consequences of these destructive agents through rapid medical diagnosis; (5) improvement in the capability to identify organisms and chemical agents in order to quickly identify and provide the appropriate medical treatment to minimize the morbidity and mortality from a chemical or biological agent; (6) enhancement of medical and epidemiological public health activities to be prepared to deal with the public health consequences of a terrorist attack; and (7) creation and activation of four metropolitan strike teams trained to meet the needs of patients in high risk communities with health problems related to weapons of mass destruction. Furthermore, implementation of this plan will provide the following benefits:

- promote coordinated planning of the integrated federal family of health and medical responders with state and local first responders;
- develop training and exercise materials;
- form integrated teams of first responders with emphasis on pre-hospital care, including triage of patients, decontamination of patients, treatment of patients, and, as appropriate, patient evacuation;
- develop public health advisories and repositories of information for use in crisis;
- augment the infrastructure of the Centers for Disease Control and Prevention, the Food and Drug Administration, and the National Institutes of Health to rapidly identify chemical and biological agents;
- augment the federal first responder capability to ensure technical assistance and rapid deployment of the NDMS; and
- ensure sufficient supplies of medicines and vaccines to meet the potential needs.

## Conclusion

This is an important and large mission. To do less would be a disservice to the American people. If the budget travails of the last year are any guide, the future implementation of this plan is uncertain. But if the strong interest of key leaders in the executive and legislative branches persists, there is every reason to believe that the nation will make great strides in addressing deficiencies in its medical response to terrorist attacks with chemical and biological agents.

# HAS THE TABOO
# BEEN BROKEN?

BRAD ROBERTS

The prospect of terrorist attacks employing chemical or biological weapons (CBW) has achieved sudden interest in the wake of the Aum Shinrikyo's attack on the Tokyo subway system in March 1995. Among analysts and academics, interest has focused on achieving a better understanding of the factors leading to such attacks. Among policymakers in the United States and abroad, interest has focused on strengthening counterterrorism responses. There is also a strong general interest in predictions of the future likelihood and magnitude of such attacks.

This monograph has sought to calibrate the CBW terrorism problem. Our goal was to probe beyond the hysteria that has gripped many to come to deeper insights into analytical and policy questions. Our method was to disaggregate the problem, examine each of its pieces in turn, and test some propositions about each. This closing chapter draws together key conclusions, arguments, and implications. Its focus is that fundamental disparity noted in the introduction—the disparity between prediction and experience. Many observers have predicted a growing number of CBW terrorist acts, given the relative technical ease with which such agents can be acquired, produced, and used. But the Aum attack stands out as the only use of such agents aimed at indiscriminate, mass destruction. Understanding this disparity is at the core of understanding the CBW terrorism problem.

More specifically, we set out to answer four fundamental questions. Was 1995 a watershed year? How important are loosening constraints on terrorist use of chemical and biological weapons? Has the taboo been broken? Having thus calibrated the problem, how do we calibrate the policy response? These questions are not, of course, separate and discrete. But the method has been productive.

# WAS 1995
# A WATERSHED YEAR?

Many pundits have argued that the attacks in Tokyo and Oklahoma City signal a new era in terrorism, one marked by more massively destructive and indiscriminate attacks with heretofore taboo weaponry. Is this proposition valid? If so, why? If not, why not?

The Tokyo subway attack was in many ways an unprecedented attack. Chemical agents have not previously been used in large scale attacks aimed at indiscriminate casualties. The fact that the agents were produced by the sect in their own production facility, in a relatively short period of time, and with resources they found easy to acquire illustrates the ease with which such an organization can perpetrate such acts.[1]

The bombing in Oklahoma City has reinforced the perception that terrorism is taking on new dimensions. Although neither chemical nor biological agents were employed, a great many deaths were caused in an attack aimed at indiscriminate carnage. The ease with which the perpetrators acquired the materials for their bomb and assembled and delivered it attest to the growing concern about technical access.

The perception was further reinforced by the unfolding trial of those involved in the bombing of the World Trade Center in New York a couple of years earlier. That trial revealed the existence of a militant group of Islamic extremists waging an armed jihad on a United States whose power they see as corrupt.[2] It may in fact have been a failed chemical attack as well.[3]

This view of America besieged by a new threat took root not least because of the particular historical moment in which these events occurred. With the passing of the Cold War and of the momentary interest in "a new world order," pundits have spoken with growing frequency of a new world disorder. More specifically, it was increasingly common in this period to hear the coming decades described as an era of civil wars waged by ruthless groups intent on ethnic cleansing. Weapons proliferation had also emerged as a major security challenge of the post-cold war era. This view of emerging chaos at the global level fit well with the sense of vulnerability created by the incidents cited above. The concurrent outbreaks of the Ebola virus combined with concerns about the effects of global warming on the human ecosystem—especially its disease propensities—inflamed these concerns.[4]

Thus we should be reticent about embracing unquestioningly the notion that 1995 was a watershed year and that the noted terrorist events are the harbinger of a new wave of terrorism employing weapons of mass destruction. As Joe Pilat has noted, major terrorist incidents such as these have always been deemed imminent and inevitable by some pundits.[5] The great rarity of such attacks does not preclude their possibility in the future. But the fact that a small handful of events clustered together in this way, with one or perhaps two of them involving an unconventional agent, cannot be taken as a clear harbinger.

Moreover, the historical record is a bit more variegated than commonly assumed. Both chemical and biological agents have been used by non-state actors for a variety of purposes over the years. One study records 244 such incidents between World War I and the present in 26 countries, 168 of which utilized chemical agents, 33 biological ones, and the remainder unidentified materials. Of those episodes, 60 percent entailed the actual use of agents and 30 percent only the threat to use (the remainder related to acquisition). The study employs a very broad definition of CB terrorism and covers incidents such as the Tylenol poisonings of 1982 and 1986, the mercury poisoning of Israeli citrus in 1978, and the salmonella poisonings perpetrated by the Rajneesh cult in Oregon in 1984, aimed at turning a local election in its favor. Only 25 percent of the surveyed episodes involved political motives, with the rest perpetrated by criminals, psychotics, and hostile employees, among others.[6]

Furthermore, the impact of the Tokyo attack has often been misunderstood. Its aim was indiscriminate casualties, but its effects were very limited. Few people died, in contrast to the many hundreds or thousands who might have died in different circumstances. The attack was chemical, but it was not mass destruction. Moreover, the attack was not an isolated event, coming as it did as the culmination of a series of attacks by the sect; the subway attack itself was in fact predicted by a CBACI analyst.[7]

The primary significance of the events of 1995 should be understood not in terms of what they reveal about terrorist propensities but for what they reveal about U.S. vulnerabilities. They brought into a harsh light the ease with which terrorists can target the American public and American institutions as well as the virtual absence of the preparations necessary to respond to terrorist attacks with chemical and biological agents. The primary lesson of 1995 is that American vulnerabilities must be minimized.[8]

# HOW IMPORTANT ARE LOOSENING CONSTRAINTS?

With events concentrating attention on U.S. vulnerabilities, analysts and policymakers then faced the challenge of bringing into better focus the nature of the CBW terrorist problem and the necessary and appropriate means to redress vulnerabilities. This focusing process was not helped by the prior lack of interest attached to the CBW terrorism subject. Nor has it been assisted by reactions to vulnerabilities evident in past years that have alternated between complacency and hysteria.

As noted in the introduction, to the extent there has been any thinking about the threat of terrorism using weapons of mass destruction, most of it has focused on the nuclear issue.[9] Chemical and biological weapons have typically been treated as a lesser-included challenge—as if somehow the technical and political barriers to nuclear use are the same as those to the use of CBW. And to the extent they have been singled out for analysis on their own terms, the ease with which such weapons might be acquired and used, relative to nuclear ones, has received primary attention. Much of the writing on chemical and biological terrorism thus has a somewhat apocalyptic tone to it, as authors conclude that with weakening constraints the use of such weapons will become increasingly frequent and increasingly destructive.[10]

To validate or probe beyond this assumption, we posed the following questions: What are those constraints? Are they in fact weakening? If so, what are the implications of those changes? Analysts have identified two primary types of constraints on the use of weapons of mass destruction by terrorists. One type is technical, the other is political.

There is little doubt that technical factors related to the use of chemical and biological weapons are far less restrictive than those related to the use of nuclear weapons. Chemical and biological weapons are easier to produce than nuclear weapons, especially for groups that must acquire not just production technologies but also precursor materials as well as the requisite expertise. Moreover, the proliferation of chemical and biological weapons to a growing number of countries increases the likelihood that the materials, technologies, and expertise necessary to the production and use of chemical and biological weapons will be available for non-state actors.[11] The widespread availability of the basic recipes for CBW agents are readily accessible, not least on the Internet, and the ongoing diffusion of dual-use commercial technologies suited also to the production of chemical and biological warfare agents only magnifies this problem. The collapse of the Soviet Union has had a similar impact, as James Adams has observed, by creating new networks of supply and expertise among Russian crime syndicates and the weapons programs of both Russia and the developing world.[12]

That the production and use of chemical and biological weapons are technically easier than the production and use of a nuclear device does not also imply that technical considerations are irrelevant to the considerations of a terrorist.[13] Chemical warfare agents may be difficult to procure or produce in quantities and purities sufficient to generate large casualties. The seed stock for biological agents may be relatively easy to acquire, but turning seed stock into deliverable biological warfare agents is a problem that has required a good deal of time and money by those few states that have pursued offensive biological warfare programs. Dispersal of BW agents in the densities and sizes necessary for lethal effect is not easy.[14] Moreover, different targets are susceptible to attack with different types of agents, with cities and ports providing very different target characteristics from specific facilities or individuals. Both chemical and biological agents are risky to the terrorist working with them, even more so than the conventional explosives that are their usual stock in trade. Successfully identifying and resolving all of the technical factors associated with the effective use of CBW agents requires a breadth of expertise, and a capacity to test unnoticed, that is beyond the reach of many terrorists and terrorist organizations. The Aum's largely ineffective attack, despite its scientific and technical acumen, large resources, and field testing, is suggestive of these challenges.

Moreover, chemical and biological agents ought to be unappealing to terrorists looking for immediate, dramatic effects. As Brian Jenkins has argued, "terrorist incidents have a finite quality—an assassination, a bombing, a handful of deaths, and that is the end of the episode. And the terrorists retain control. This is quite different from initiating an event that offers no bang but instead produces indiscriminate deaths and lingering illness, over which the terrorists would have little control."[15]

Thus, it is hardly surprising that some analysts of these technical barriers to terrorist use of CBW conclude that the loosening technical constraints associated with proliferation, technology diffusion, and the Internet do not imply that terrorists will find it easy to acquire, develop, or successfully employ such weapons regularly. Rather, the effect of changing technical constraints seems to be to influence the choices of terrorists in one direction or another. Few terrorists are likely to utilize the latest high technology to produce novel designer biological or chemical agents, even if this is now technically possible; instead, the ready availability of low-technology materials and the proven appeal of cyanide and similar poisons implies a preference for lower-tech approaches. The terrorists most likely to make successful use of CBW agents are those able to draw on the resources of a well-funded state chemical and biological warfare program; but these are precisely the terrorists least likely to use such weapons (for reasons explained below).

In sum, technical barriers are indeed declining. But they've never been particularly high. Nor have they entirely disappeared. The fact that terrorists have made such limited use of chemical and biological weapons suggests that barriers other than technical are important as well. This points to the role of political constraints.

As Brian Jenkins has argued, "if murder and mayhem were their primary objective, terrorists would certainly have killed many more people."[16] That they have chosen not to kill more people must have something to do with their choices not to use weapons of mass destruction. But why would violent terrorists willing to kill indiscriminately opt not to kill large numbers of people?

The answer has to do with the political purposes driving many terrorist actors and organizations. To quote Jenkins again: "The capability to kill on a grand scale must be balanced against the fear of alienating perceived constituents (a population that terrorists invariably overestimate), provoking widespread revulsion, and unleashing government crackdowns that have public approval." [17] Most terrorists are motivated by what they believe to be legitimate political goals and utilize violence in ways intended to achieve those goals. Their use of violence must therefore be carefully calculated. It must inflict enough pain on society to gain a hearing for their cause, a seat at the table, or a political concession of some kind. But it must not be so painful as to exceed the tolerance of society, eliminating support for its goals and resulting in decisive punishment and retribution by the government, as encouraged by an enraged and fearful public. Jenkins invokes the analogy of the volume control knob to explain how terrorists calibrate and recalibrate their use of violence in the light of changing societal and political circumstances—loud enough to be heard but not too loud to loosen the bonds that prevent people from reacting strongly.[18]

Unfortunately, such political sensitivities may not always operate to constrain such acts of violence. Terrorists may be less concerned with alienating key constituencies if the targets of their violence are overseas or among the populations of states that have been dehumanized through sustained ideological propaganda, as Jerrold Post has argued.[19] Moreover, as argued below, some terrorist groups do not appear motivated by a desire to extract some type of political concession from a state or group of states. Additionally, the number of such groups appears to be increasing.

Ron Purver has helped to put this debate about constraints into perspective. His comprehensive analysis of the literature of chemical and biological terrorism uncovers a set of nearly a dozen factors that have been defined as barriers to terrorist use of such weapons. These include both operational constraints and the fear of alienating supporters noted above. In addition he cites the uncontrollable character of the use of CBW agents, the fear of terrorists for their own personal safety in working with the agents, the unwelcomed indiscriminate effects of their use, moral qualms, the fact that such weapons appear to be unnecessary to the achievement of many terrorist goals, restraint by state sponsors, and the absence of demands for which such threats could conceivably be useful.[20] He concludes that some of these factors are losing their cogency while others still have a constraining effect.[21]

Thus, the cumulative effect of changing technical and political constraints remains ambiguous. But a worst-case analysis is not warranted by the available facts. The likelihood of apocalyptic use as the result of declining barriers has been overstated. Technical constraints remain, but they do not work quite as conceived by many observers. Political constraints remain as well, at least insofar as the heretofore most common types of terrorism remain predominant.

# IS THE TABOO REALLY BROKEN?

If the effect of loosening technical and political constraints is uncertain, what other factors are likely to bear on the future propensity of terrorists to use chemical and biological weapons?

Historically, these weapons have been subject to a kind of taboo. Their use has been seen as especially reprehensible and unacceptable at many different times in history and by many different cultures. How is this taboo at risk? On whom is it operative? Has it in fact been broken? In what ways might it not have broken?

The taboo against chemical and biological weapons has been threatened, it is argued, by Aum's use of sarin nerve gas in its attacks, because terrorists are mimics. Once one group uses a new tool of violence, others tend to follow, whether in copycat attacks or in a more calculated drive to continue to command media and public attention. Thus if Aum has done what was forbidden, others are sure to follow, goes the argument.

This is too simple a view of the problem. A more nuanced understanding requires an analytical distinction between traditional terrorist actors (individuals or groups) and new terrorist actors. The taboo is likely to operate quite differently on these different actors.[22]

Of the traditional terrorist actors, there are essentially three types. One type utilizes violence to demand a seat at the political table and to compel respect for a cause. As argued above, such actors must calibrate the level of violence they employ—enough to underline their cause but not too much to undermine their legitimacy. This is arguably why organizations such as the Palestine Liberation Organization and the Irish Republican Army have seen weapons of mass destruction as counterproductive of their aims.

A second type of actor utilizes violence to invoke an overreaction by the state, in the hope that this will cause the people to rise up and cast off a corrupt, authoritarian state. This is the terrorism of the Red Army Faction and the Baader-Meinhof Gang, for example. Groups such as these also have had to calibrate the level of violence. By and large, they have failed to do so, creating more sympathy for a state crackdown on their behavior than for their cause.

A third type is the state-sponsored actor. The violent ways of terrorists are exploited and manipulated by foreign powers to gain political leverage within a state or region in the service of a global anti-status quo campaign. The violence that they employ must also be calibrated by both the terrorist group, fearful of being tracked down and eliminated, and by the sponsoring state, fearful of being attacked in retribution for acts clearly attributed to it. Weapons of mass destruction have, so far at least, been seen as counterproductive for such terrorists.

All three types of terrorist must carefully calculate thresholds of pain and tolerance in the targeted society if their use of violence is to be successful in reaping political gains. It is noteworthy that none has seen nuclear, biological, or chemical weapons as useful to its purposes—especially given that many state sponsors of terror are also countries of key CBW proliferation concern. This suggests that important barriers to future use remain in place. The Aum attack is not likely to be seen as having eliminated the need for calculating thresholds of pain and tolerance—indeed, if anything, the attack might be read by such terrorists as demonstrating the firm state reactions that are likely to be provoked by such incidents.

There is at least one important caveat to this assessment. Terrorists seem increasingly to prefer indiscriminate types of attacks, as witnessed in recent years by the growing use of car bombings and suicide bombings in public places. This may contribute to greater interest among traditional terrorist groups in chemical and/or biological weapons.[23]

In contrast to these so-called traditional terrorist actors, whose use of violence is largely for political purposes, the Tokyo, Oklahoma City, and New York attacks seem to signal the emergence of new types of terrorists motivated by different concerns and interests. They may not be bound by the political and technical constraints that, so far at least, have served to inhibit CBW terrorism. The essential questions are whether there will be more such actors and whether CBW weapons will appeal to them. Again, there are three primary types of this emerging form of terrorism.

The first type is state-sponsored terrorism in war or near-war situations. Such terrorists might use one or a few attacks with weapons of mass destruction to sow fear among the American public, hoping thus to generate political pressures in Congress that will induce the president to avoid military confrontation with the sponsoring state or to back down from such confrontation once begun. This form of terrorism may of course reflect a fundamental misreading of the American public, which is more likely to be enraged by such acts and to seek prompt and decisive removal of the offending regime than to cower in fear. For these terrorist purposes, nuclear weapons seem likely to appear unattractive (given the certainty of the response they would evoke from the United States), whereas chemical or biological weapons may appear less so, especially considering the plausible case that the sponsoring state might make in denying responsibility for any sudden outbreak of disease in the United States. This is the terrorism feared by the United States during the United Nations effort to expel Iraq from Kuwait and that it continues to fear as it contemplates possible major regional contingencies against rogue states armed with NBC weapons. A variant on this type of terrorism might be the use of such weapons in attacks on the populations of U.S. allies, in the belief that those allies would pressure the United States to capitulate.

The second type is terrorism motivated by the desire to strike a crippling blow against a hated enemy. Such terrorism may well be the act of one or two individuals and not of a group or state. Possible targets and purposes are numerous. These might be acts of "sacred terror" against symbols of corrupt power on earth.[24] They might be strikes against despised ethnic groups. They might be calculated attempts to disrupt the economy or political institutions of decaying imperialist states, in the hope of speeding their collapse. Or they might be acts of radical paranoia, aimed at fanciful enemies. They might also be acts of vengeance or righteousness, aimed not so much at crippling the target as at getting even. This is the terrorism of the Aum, of the radical right, of hate groups, of Rwandan war lords. The fact that the CBW terrorism problem is emerging at the end of not just a century but a millennium raises questions about whether groups or individuals motivated by end-of-history beliefs might not use weapons of mass destruction to speed the new era. For any of these purposes, chemical and biological weapons might have a special appeal as particularly insidious and, in the case of infectious biological agents, essentially uncontrollable. In the United States in particular, the apparent interest of the militia movement and other elements of the radical right in poisons is an especially worrisome matter, although the predilection of these same communities for the traditional guns and bombs of lawless America may minimize the risks that they will turn their interest in poisons into use in military-style attacks.[25]

The third type is hardly terrorism at all but it merits consideration in this analysis. This is the act of venal criminality brought to new heights of violence by the new availability of the scientific and technical expertise of mass destruction. These acts may hardly be considered as terrorism per se, but rather as acts of extortion or simple mass murder. But they could well induce public terror, even if the actor did not intend to exploit terror for political purposes. They could also have some spillover effects on terrorists, if they are spectacularly successful or spectacularly failures.

Of course, none of these types of terrorism is really new. But organizations and individuals willing to exploit violence for these purposes appear to be growing in number in the 1990s. Whether this perception is statistically sound remains undetermined. Moreover, people fear that those numbers will grow in the decades ahead if developed countries suffer further social decay and if developing countries continue to suffer civil and international war (in addition to social decay). For all three types, calculations of pain thresholds and tolerances seem unlikely. Only for those in the first category is the use of violence aimed at extracting political concessions. For the latter two especially, chemical and biological weapons may seem attractive. They will certainly be technically within the reach of most or all terrorists.

So has the taboo been broken? The answer is no and yes. For traditional terrorist actors, important barriers remain to the use of weapons of mass destruction, as such weapons are fundamentally counterproductive of their intended goals. Even new groups that form in future years to press claims of legitimacy seem unlikely to embrace such weapons. But for nontraditional terrorist actors, the taboo may not be relevant.

# WHAT ARE THE APPROPRIATE TASKS OF POLICY?

The CBW terrorism problem is then a challenge with quite specific dimensions. The emergence of new individuals or groups willing to use violence for purposes other than traditional political ones raises a large question about the future. The diffusion of the materials, technology, and expertise necessary for the production and use of chemical and biological agents magnifies these concerns. On the other hand, there are many countervailing factors germane to the prediction of the future prevalence and severity of CB terrorist attacks. Both technical and political factors will inhibit future recourse to chemical or biological modes of attack. The threatened use of such weapons may increase in frequency, but actual use seems likely to remain limited. Moreover, massively destructive attacks appear to be the least likely mode of attack. This view of the problem implies that policy must walk a fine line between doing enough to redress existing vulnerabilities without overreacting to the problem. As yet, there is no evidence to suggest that a wave of mass destruction terrorism is about to be unleashed on the United States. But this does not preclude singular events, including those generating large casualties.

With this characterization of the problem in mind, what then are the appropriate tasks of policy? Rather than enumerate a detailed list of specific action steps, where do national priorities lie? What can policy reasonably be expected to contribute to amelioration of this problem, and what can it not be expected to contribute? And what are the future risks of failing now to implement an appropriate agenda?

It is not necessary to begin from scratch. In the year after the Tokyo attack, the administration and the Congress have cobbled together an agenda for dealing with the threat of CBW terrorism. It is embodied in the Counterterrorism Act of 1996 and Presidential Decision Directive 38 (on terrorism). That agenda encompasses many elements. It promotes medical preparedness in cities of special terrorism risk. It strengthens governmental coordination within and among local, state, and federal entities, as well as counterterrorism cooperation between the United

States and other countries. It bolsters the capacity of the intelligence community to identify future CBW threats. In all of these, it builds on existing foundations of medical and emergency preparedness, law enforcement, diplomacy, and intelligence.[26]

The key question is whether this agenda will be invested with the leadership and funding necessary to sustain its work over the coming years. Critical elements have been hotly contested in partisan fashion, while others have suffered from the federal budget crunch. Key leaders in both the executive and legislative branches are stepping out of the picture, and whether new ones will emerge remains, at this writing, an open question. Kathleen Bailey has rightly observed that there can never be enough money to do everything that might seem useful, and thus that scarce dollars must be targeted on those projects likely to pay the highest dividends.[27]

The following additional points bear on the future of U.S. policy vis-à-vis chemical and biological terrorism.

First, *relative to the nuclear problem*, a great deal more emphasis should be paid to managing the consequences of a chemical or biological terrorist attack than to attempting to prevent or to defuse an attack as it unfolds. In the nuclear domain, the prospects for an act of terrorism can be significantly reduced by sustaining and enhancing the control on fissile materials in Russia and elsewhere. In contrast, controlling the materials of chemical or biological terrorism is impossible, although there are important benefits to be reaped from the destruction of chemical weapons arsenals now sprinkled throughout more than 20 countries and of the biological arsenals of undetermined number.[28] Similarly, detecting and interdicting terrorist supplies of such materials is likely to be considerably easier in the nuclear than in the chemical and biological domains.

This implies an emphasis on consequence management. The efficient management of the consequences of a nuclear attack may well be beyond the capacity of emergency responders, but many improvements can be made in the capacity of those responders to deal with chemical and biological contingencies.[29] This is not to deny the potential value of improved intelligence and stronger materials controls in helping to prevent or defuse chemical and biological crises. Moreover, the routine and ongoing work of health and environmental protection can help to expose the work of groups such as Aum and bring law enforcement to bear before a terrorist event produces consequences that require managing.[30]

Second, policy that fails to address the normative context is policy that will be virtually irrelevant to the future CB challenge. As Brendon Hammer has argued, the relative prominence of chemical and biological terrorism in the century ahead will be determined by social forces as well as technical and political forces—specifically, by whether terrorists, their constituencies, and the states with which they compete will see chemical and biological weapons as an acceptable, increasingly conventional form of warfare.[31] If CB proliferation prevails over international arms control efforts, and states turn increasingly to the development and use of CBW, Hammer argues, then terrorists will reckon the use of CBW to have become more acceptable and may use it with less fear of alienating a constituency. In this view, maintenance through nonproliferation and arms control of strong state-level norms against the use of CBW will stop undermining of norms against CBW at the societal level, and will thereby reduce the likelihood of CB terrorism.

Brian Jenkins has reinforced this view: "Why would terrorists choose nuclear weapons over chemical or biological weapons...? In several ways, these weapons are less attractive. Terrorists imitate governments, and nuclear weapons are in the arsenals of the world's major powers. That makes them 'legitimate.' Chemical and biological weapons also may be found in the arsenals of many nations, but their use has been widely condemned by public opinion and proscribed by treaty, although in recent years the constraints against their use seem to be eroding."[32]

This points to two tasks—one at the grassroots level and one at the international level. At the grassroots level it would seem highly desirable simultaneously to teach those students being taught technologies specifically applicable to CW and BW production that international law and broader morality dictates that they not turn their skills to the production of such weapons. Thus universities and other schools could be asked to require that students in relevant areas of chemistry and biology also take and pass a short course on legal and moral obligations inter alia with respect to CBW production. Such a course requirement might have made a difference in Japan, for example, to the capacity of the Aum Shinrikyo sect to convince postgraduate chemists to make nerve agents for use on the Tokyo subway.

The other task is strengthening of the global regime for the control of chemical and biological weapons.[33] The Biological and Toxin Weapons Convention of 1972 remains a regime of suspect quality and utility, with large, unresolved questions about the compliance of both minor and major powers; strengthening the regime with the addition of compliance provisions—and using those provisions to secure compliance—should pay dividends in reinvigorating the anti-BW norm. The Chemical Weapons Convention of 1993 remains a hostage of events since its signing, with entry into force and its final disposition still uncertain. This latter regime in particular has a number of attributes relevant to the terrorism problem beyond the normative one.[34]

Third, it is useful to conceive of the consequences of a crisis of CB terrorism poorly prepared for and poorly met by the U.S. government. There would be human consequences, to be sure, of casualties that might not have been suffered with adequate preparations. But there would be political consequences as well. An attack that inflicted major casualties on American citizens could unleash a rage that would propel the United States to a sharp reply, whether in search of swift justice at home or revenge if perpetrated from abroad. These might well be actions the United States would later regret. Among them are the draconian restrictions on political liberties that might be deemed necessary in a moment of particular vulnerability. Being ready—and looking ready—may minimize these pressures to act in such ways. It may also help to deter such an event in the first place, by fostering an image of the United States that will not be pitched into terror by the poisonous behavior of individual miscreants.

# CONCLUSIONS

The problem of chemical and biological terrorism is here to stay. It will be around so long as chemical and biological weapons exist. But the facts that they have been around for millennia and that they have not proven to be favored instruments of particularly willful and violent individuals and groups augur well for the future.

There is a risk that the CBW terrorism problem will be excessively hyped, especially in the wake of individual events. Blowing the threat out of proportion damages our ability to calibrate the necessary policy response. Alternatively, the complacency that long characterized U.S. policy seems unlikely to reappear any time soon. But something like complacency may prevail, if the existing counterterrorism program is eroded through a shortage of political commitment and leadership.

With only a little luck, the United States should find that the use of chemical and biological warfare agents by terrorists will remain rare and unlikely. With only a bit of skill and diligence, it should find that its vulnerabilities can be addressed in constructive ways. Minimizing those vulnerabilities, however, requires looking beyond the counterterrorism policy agenda of the moment to the larger normative context and the way values, technology, and society will evolve and intersect in the decades ahead.

# NOTES

1. For more on the Aum Shinrikyo attack, see the hearings conducted by the U.S. Senate Subcommittee on Investigations, Committee on Governmental Affairs, March 13, 20, 27, 1996. See also D. W. Brackett, *Holy Terror: Armageddon in Tokyo* (New York: Weatherhill, Inc., 1996) and David E. Kaplan and Andrew Marshall, *The Cult at the End of the World* (New York: Crown, 1996).
2. For more on this, see Steven Emerson, "Terrorism and the Middle East Peace Process: the Origins and Activities of Hamas in the United States," testimony to the U.S. Senate Subcommittee on the Near East and South Asia, Committee on Foreign Relations, March 19, 1996.
3. In his sentencing statement, the judge who presided at the trial of the bombers indicated that the explosive device had included chemical agents that burned in the explosion instead of disseminating throughout the building as intended.
4. See, for example, Laurie Garrett, *The Coming Plague: Newly Emerging Diseases in a World Out of Balance* (New York: Farrer, Straus and Giroux, 1994). For a more

historical perspective on the relationship between the human community and the disease pool, see William H. McNeill, *Plagues and Peoples* (New York: Doubleday, 1977).

5.  Joseph F. Pilat, "Prospects for NBC Terrorism after Tokyo," in this volume.

6.  The study was prepared by Harvey J. McGeorge. An early version was published as "Chemical and Biological Terrorism: Analyzing the Problem," in *The ASA* [Applied Science and Analysis, Inc.] *Newsletter*, No. 42, June 16, 1994, pp. 1, 12-13. An updated version was presented orally to the CBACI conference on April 29, 1996. McGeorge is president of the Public Safety Group of Woodbridge, Va.

7.  Kyle B. Olson, "The Matsumoto Incident: Sarin Poisoning in a Japanese Residential Community," CBACI, February 1995.

8.  This was the key argument made by John Sopko in his presentation to the CBACI conference. Sopko is a member of the staff of the U.S. Senate's Permanent Subcommittee on Investigations, in which capacity he was responsible for directing the Senate's investigation into the Aum attack and the hearings on the national security threat posed by the proliferation of nuclear, chemical, and biological weapons and terrorism (hearings dated March 13, 20, 27, 1996).

9.  This literature includes the following illustrative items: Paul Leventhal and Yonah Alexander, eds., *Preventing Nuclear Terrorism* (Lexington, Mass.: Lexington, 1987); Brian M. Jenkins, "Will Terrorists Go Nuclear?" in Walter Laqueur and Yonah Alexander, eds., *The Terrorism Reader* (New York: Penguin, 1987), pp. 350-357; Andrew Loehmer, "The Nuclear Dimension," in Paul Wilkinson, ed., *Technology and Terrorism* (Portland, Or.: Frank Cass, 1993), pp. 48-69.

10. See for example Joseph D. Douglas, Jr., and Neil C. Livingstone, *America the Vulnerable: the Threat of Chemical/Biological Warfare, the New Shape of Terrorism and Conflict* (Lexington, Mass.: Lexington, 1987). See also Paul Bremer, "The Fight Against Super-Terrorism," prepared for a conference on "Dealing with the Spread of Nuclear Weapons," of the Netherlands Atlantic Commission, The Hague, The Netherlands, May 19, 1995, and Robert H. Kupperman and David M. Smith, "Coping With Biological Terrorism," in Brad Roberts, ed., *Biological Weapons: Weapons of the Future?* (Washington, D.C.: Center for Strategic and International Studies, 1993), pp. 35-45.

11. For a discussion of some of the connections between CBW proliferation and terrorism, see Edward M. Spiers, *Chemical and Biological Weapons: A Study of Proliferation* (London: Macmillan, 1994).

12. James Adams, "The Dangerous New World of Chemical and Biological Weapons," in this volume. Adams rightly decries the singular fixation on the consequences for nuclear proliferation of Soviet collapse, and urges greater attention to the emerging CBW problem.

13. Karl Lowe, "Analyzing Technical Constraints on Bio-Terrorism: Are They Still Important?" in this volume. See also Wayman C. Mullins, "An Overview and Analysis of Nuclear, Biological, and Chemical Terrorism: The Weapons, Strategies and Solutions to a Growing Problem," *American Journal of Criminal Justice*, Vol. XVI, No. 2 (1992), pp. 95-119.

14. This point has been made by many analysts, including Loehmer, "The Nuclear Dimension," p. 63.

15. Jenkins, "Will Terrorists Go Nuclear?", p. 356.

16. Jenkins, "Understanding the Link between Motives and Methods," in this volume.
17. Jenkins, "Will Terrorists Go Nuclear?", p. 353. His view is echoed by others. See for example, Elliott Hurwitz, "Terrorists and Chemical/Biological Weapons," *Naval War College Review*, Vol. 35, No. 3 (May-June 1982), pp. 36-40. See also Jeffrey D. Simon, "Terrorists and the Potential Use of Biological Weapons: A Discussion of Possibilities," R-3771-AFMIC (Santa Monica, Calif.: RAND, December 1989).
18. Jenkins, "Understanding the Link between Motives and Methods."
19. Jerrold M. Post, "Prospects for Nuclear Terrorism: Psychological Motivations and Constraints," in Leventhal and Alexander, *Preventing Nuclear Terrorism*, pp. 91-103. Post also argues that group-think propensities will operate within terrorist groups leading them to dysfunctional choices. Jenkins also emphasizes the significant role of group dynamics, though he notes the importance many groups attach to maintaining cohesion, leading them to choose not to take high risk actions.
20. Ron Purver, "Understanding Past Non-Use of CBW," in this volume. His chapter draws on a larger study, entitled "Chemical and Biological Terrorism: The Threat According to the Open Literature" (Ottawa: Canadian Security Intelligence Service, June 1995).
21. For a useful discussion of whether and how moral barriers have influenced past terrorist behavior, see Albert Bandura, "Mechanisms of Moral Disengagement," in Walter Reich, ed., *Origins of Terrorism* (Cambridge, Mass: Cambridge University Press and Woodrow Wilson International Center for Scholars, 1990), pp. 161-191.
22. The following argument draws heavily on Brad Roberts, "Terrorism and Weapons of Mass Destruction: Has the Taboo Been Broken?" in *Politics and the Life Sciences* (September 1996), pp. 32-33.
23. Bruce Hoffman, "Terrorist Targeting: Tactics, Trends, and Potentialities," in Wilkinson, *Technology and Terrorism*, pp. 12-29.
24. David C. Rapoport, "Sacred Terror," in Reich, ed., *Origins of Terrorism*, pp. 103-130.
25. For more on this point, see Anthony Fainberg, "Debating Policy Priorities and Implications," in this volume.
26. This summary draws on a detailed presentation to the CBACI conference by Michael Jakub of the Office of the Coordinator for Counterterrorism in the Department of State. Further details can be found in the chapters in this volume by Mssrs. Pilat, Fainberg, Tucker, and Young.
27. From her oral presentation to the April 29 CBACI conference. Dr. Bailey is on the staff of the Lawrence Livermore National Laboratory and is the author of *Doomsday Weapons in the Hands of the Many: The Arms Control Challenge of the 90s* (Urbana, Ill.: University of Illinois Press, 1991).
28. It should be recalled that some terrorists groups have tried to steal biological agents rather than make their own. In 1970, for example, the leftist Weather Underground was discovered to have been planning to steal such agents from Ft. Detrick, Maryland. See Mullins, "An Overview and Analysis," p. 100.
29. For a detailed comparative analysis of the requirements of access denial, interdiction, crisis management, and consequence management in comparative nuclear, biological, and chemical terms, see the summary paper of the conference on Nuclear, Biological, and Chemical Weapons Proliferation and Terrorism, jointly sponsored by the Los Alamos National Laboratory and the Center for Science and Interna-

tional Affairs, Harvard University, May 23, 1996.

30. I am indebted to Seth Carus for this point, who notes the many opportunities missed by Japanese officials to "manage" the Aum threat before it began to test and ultimately use its chemical agents.

31. Hammer is a counselor at the Embassy of Australia. The comments noted here are drawn from his oral presentation to the CBACI conference.

32. Jenkins, "Will Terrorists Go Nuclear?" p. 355.

33. I am again indebted to Seth Carus, who notes in reaction to this line of argument that high-level, state-to-state diplomacy on CBW weaponry has sometimes stimulated the interest of both states and non-state actors in such weaponry. The Aum's interest in CBW has a strong basis, for example, in the revelations about Iraq's capabilities.

34. These include: (1) requiring states to enact laws criminalizing the production of, or attempted production of, chemical weapons; (2) requiring states to control the production of chemical weapons; (3) alerting chemical industries to the danger that their products may be misused; (4) creating national and international agencies that can serve as resources in the fight against terrorism; (5) discouraging states from assisting or protecting chemical terrorists; (6) assisting states that are the victims of actual or threatened terrorist attacks; (7) eliminating national stockpiles of chemical weapons that might otherwise fall into the hands of terrorists; and (8) providing a forum for discussing chemical terrorism-related problems. R. Justin Smith, "Chemical Terrorism and the Chemical Weapons Convention," working paper prepared for the 3rd workshop of the Pugwash study group on the Implementation of the Chemical and Biological Weapons Conventions, Noordwijk, The Netherlands, May 1995, pp.19-21.